Medicine Men
EXTREME APPALACHIAN DOCTORING

Carolyn Jourdan

In this book Smoky Mountain dialect is rendered as it sounds. Appalachian speech is poetic and musical. It's sung as much as spoken, so a significant portion of the meaning is conveyed in the cadences and tones.

Dialect is used in conversation by people of all levels of education and intelligence, so no apostrophes will highlight dropped g's or word variants, as if they are errors. For the same reason, the local grammar is retained, as are phrases in dialect such as "in the floor" instead of "on the floor."

This was done to enable the reader to experience Smoky Mountain life and language intimately, as an insider would.

Designed by Karen Key

Printed in the United States of America

E-Book ISBN-13: 978-0-9885643-0-5

Printed Book ISBN-13: 978-0-9885643-1-2

Table of Contents

After ***Heart in the Right Place*** was published I got thousands of requests for more real life stories of madcap medical mayhem, so I decided to publish this little collection because I believe sweet-natured comedy is the most healing force on earth.

In the Smokies, doctors stand toe-to-toe with the dragon and work right in its very breath. But I've never heard any of them act like the doctors you see on television. In the world of old-school Appalachian doctoring there's no team of experts standing by to help. There aren't any exotic machines. And there's usually no money.

These stories are all true. The star is nearly always a lone physician armed with whatever he can cram into a small black leather bag, but sometimes it's a patient, or a pharmacist, or the doctor's wife. Country doctors are men with nerves of steel and hearts of gold. They're saints who walk among us. My father is one of them.

In addition to the stories from my own family, a dozen other Southern Appalachian Highland doctors graciously added their own most memorable medical moments to this anthology.

This wide-ranging collection of jewels covers seventy-five years of medicine, from 1930 to 2005. Each of the doctors in this book practiced for over fifty years.

It's a wild and emotional ride. I hope you'll enjoy your sojourn into a world where no one is turned away and the most important qualifications are courage, kindness, patience, and a terrific sense of humor.

Now when the sun was setting, all they that had any sick with divers diseases brought them unto him; and he laid his hands on every one of them, and healed them.
Luke 4:40

Prologue

At the pinnacle of what I used to think of as my career, a family emergency required that I abandon my fast-lane Washington lifestyle and return home to the Smoky Mountains of East Tennessee.

My mother had fallen ill and the family needed a temporary replacement for her as the receptionist in my father's rural medical office. I was assured that I would only be needed for a couple of days, so how could I say no?

I could handle my mother's job without too much trouble because I was practically raised in the office. For most of my life I'd helped out, to the extent I was able, during nights, holidays, and weekends. But when I returned after many years living away in the big city, I saw the place with new eyes.

It was a dizzying transition. In the blink of an eye, I traded forests of white marble columns and vast domes of gold leaf for more than half a million acres of colorful autumn foliage gilded by the slanting yellow rays of the late afternoon sun.

As my two-day stint stretched into weeks, months, and then years, I slowly shed my identity as a U.S. Senate lawyer, or any kind of lawyer, and became a not particularly noteworthy but deeply satisfied participant in some genuine public service, humble though it was.

No more cross-country jaunts in private jets or joyrides on nuclear submarines. It was enough to take the occasional bone-jarring sprint across the cow pasture in an antique twelve cylinder convertible Cadillac, trunk lid permanently removed so the behemoth could be used to haul hay.

It's hard to overstate the difference between a world like Washington where my colleagues and I would frequently ask each other, "Is that with a *b* or an *m*?" to clarify whether we were talking billions or mere millions, and a world where the only way some people had to get any cash at all was by foraging in the woods for walnuts during a short harvesting season.

Because money was scarce, my father treated hundreds of people for free, on some days everyone. But his patients weren't the kind to feel comfortable accepting charity, so, when they could, they'd drop by and leave off some token of thanks for his kindness. The fact that this sort of exchange has become a hackneyed stereotype doesn't take away from its charm. Sure, he got the traditional food items like fresh fruits and vegetables, whole-hog sausage and home-cured ham, beans and cornbread, fudge and divinity. But more often than not, he got paid with less predictable sorts of things.

Sometimes the gift was actually a burden, but, whatever it was, Daddy always accepted it gracefully: a tiny blue jay that had fallen out of its nest, a cardboard box containing four deodorized baby skunks, an orphaned raccoon in a boot.

He got all sorts of things: a cutting of an admired maple

tree, a twig that grew into a magnificent climbing yellow rose, a half stick of dynamite probably stolen from the mines, a rusty Confederate sword found in the woods, Indian arrowheads turned up by a plow, a handful of bungee cords scavenged from alongside the interstate, and the back half of a 1934 Chevrolet pickup truck that would "make a good trailer to haul things in."

During the four years I worked with him I got to share in the pleasure of seeing these interactions. The sweetest thing I ever saw him get was an offer of friendship from an elderly retarded man who stuttered out a shy invitation for Daddy to visit his very rural cabin where he suggested they could sit together on his porch and watch the squirrels play. He generously added to the bargain by telling Daddy, "*You* can sit in the *chair.*"

No amount of money in the world could ever outdo a deal like that.

The most unusual thing he ever got was the still-warm body of a red fox that a patient had seen get hit by a car. Daddy took the beautiful corpse to a taxidermist and then displayed the magnificent creature for decades until my mother could no longer vacuum the dust out of its thick fur.

My favorite thing he ever got paid with was given to him when I was a teenager. It was made by a ninety year old widow who was so crippled with arthritis she lived confined to only a single room of her house. Daddy made free house calls on her for many years and, in return, she sewed him a quilt. The night he brought the quilt home he gave it to me with tears in his eyes. He said he couldn't bear to look at it because of the hours of painful effort he knew it had cost her.

That lovely quilt has hung on the wall near my bed wherever I lived. It's a giant pink star on a white background. I've spent years marveling at the thousands of tiny stitches placed by the lady's gnarled fingers.

Nowadays the quilt reminds me of what a real career is all about. It's not about the direct deposit of currency from one bank account to another or dressing up and getting on C-Span while you work. It's about the one-on-one exchange of time and attention, warmth and concern.

The star quilt is a testament to a rural community, an epic poem from an old lady to my father. It says a lot about the blessings of really noticing the people around us. It says everything you'd ever need to know about love and kindness, patience and courage, and Southern lives, well lived.

"I was making a housecall on an elderly gentleman when I noticed the screen was broken out of his television set. I asked him what happened.

"He told me he'd shot it.

"'Why?' I asked.

"'I'z watchin a show when a bunch of half dressed women come out,' he said. 'I'm not havin no nekkid women paradin around inside my house!'"

Better Late Than Never

The people of the Smoky Mountains are world famous for their contentiousness. The locals seem to have a genius for mayhem, and I'm not talking exclusively about the descendants of Europeans.

Some people believe the Cherokee Indians invented biological warfare the first time they set fire to a patch of woods in the Smokies, ostensibly to clear the forest floor in a time-honored ecological practice, but also because they knew the area they'd set afire was full of poison ivy and was upwind from a pesky new settlement of white people.

This feisty disposition is not just in the humans either. The dog indigenous to the southern Appalachians is called a *Mountain Feist*, a scrappy little cur considered ounce-for-ounce to be one of the most courageous dogs around.

All this goes to show that great warriors aren't necessarily who you'd expect, as Dr. Benton told me.

"One of my most memorable patients was Mr. Sam Loveday. He was the last of the old-time mountain men. He lived right on the boundary of the Great Smoky Mountains National Park and worked a steep farm alone, mostly by hand. He always said he'd rather plow with a mule than a tractor because that way he could hear the birds sing while he worked.

"He was a quiet, solitary fellow, hardly ever left his farm. I treated him several times and found him likeable, but he never really mixed with people. He preferred a stark, self-sufficient lifestyle on his old home place. Other people would give anything to escape all that labor, but he seemed to enjoy it.

"When he was very old, very ill, and confined to bed in the hospital, I visited him every day. We talked about a lot of different things and, at some point, the topic of the military came up. I mentioned I'd served in the Marines and fought in the Korean War.

"Sam was quiet for a long time, then he said, 'I've never talked about that, but I don't guess I mind tellin you.' He told me that he'd been a Marine in World War II. He'd fought in the Pacific for years. Then he told me things he'd never spoken about to anyone.

"He said near the end of a ferocious battle for control of an island, he and one other soldier were the only remaining American survivors. And all they had left was a fifty caliber water-cooled machine gun and a great deal of ammunition. He said, 'The Japs kept comin' and comin' and comin'. And we kept shootin' and shootin' and shootin' 'til we'd shot 'em all. Then we slipped off and lived in caves 'til the Allies took the island back.

"'The Navy eventually found us and told us the Japanese had signed the surrender. As soon as I heard that I took off for home.'

"He said he'd never bothered to get properly discharged. When he'd heard the fighting was over, he'd simply *left*, hopping on the first of a long series of whatever transport seemed to be heading in the right direction. He managed to make it all the way home amid the chaos of the war's end.

"For fifty years he'd assumed he was in serious trouble for leaving without official permission, so he'd lived in isolation ever since, hiding from the Marine Corps. His brief experience of foreign lands and the hellish advances of modern machinery were more than he could stand. So he never again left the county he was born in and he never again laid his hand to anything but primitive hand tools. He relied on his farm animals for companionship.

"Now I understood why he lived like he did. He'd needed to heal himself with peace and quiet and by tending animals and growing things among his own people.

"When it became clear that Mr. Loveday was dying, I suggested to one of his neighbors that he notify the Marines, explain the situation, and ask if they might be willing to send him his service ribbons.

"The Marines agreed immediately, but they didn't just send his ribbons, they dispatched a full general and a lot of other brass to the hospital to deliver them in person.

"It turned out the Marines had indeed been looking for Mr. Loveday for a long time, but not because he was AWOL. They'd been trying to find him because he'd won a pile of medals. An honor guard stood around his hospital bed and the general conducted an official ceremony where he told the stories of Mr. Loveday's heroism. Then he pinned the medals on Sam's robe. The local newspaper ran a big article about him and the community was able to see the reclusive farmer in a whole new light.

"Sam lived for only two more days after his awards ceremony, but I know they were very good days."

"Back in the old days, most people died at home. And doctors used to help the family with customs that aren't followed nowadays. When I first started in practice, it was traditional for the doctor to be the one who placed a coin on each of the deceased's eyelids to hold them closed. And it depended on how well off the people were whether they'd hand you a nickel or a quarter to use. Some people were very poor. They'd have to scramble to come up with two coins of any kind."

Making a Doctor

Who are these people who go into rural medicine? What kind of person would want a job where they'd be on call 24/7/365 for the rest of their lives?

And what if the job frequently involved facing life-threatening emergencies with advance knowledge that you'd be lucky if you ever got paid? What on earth would make someone choose this kind of life?

In Daddy's case, when he was a small boy he asked his father to tell him about the most educated man he'd ever met. His father, a man whose formal education stopped at the 3rd grade, named the local doctor. "Doc Daniels," he said. "Doctors have to go to school longer than anybody." Based on that, Daddy decided he wanted to be a doctor.

In the course of talking with dozens of rural medical practitioners I heard a variety of other motivations. Some were raised by doctors, so they were eased naturally into their careers—doctoring was simply what the family did. But for others the decision to live a life dedicated to the health of others was made as a conscious, deliberate choice at a profound turning point in their lives.

For Dr. Andrews it happened when he was a little boy, dangerously ill with a high fever. Each time he opened his eyes during a long night of misery he was comforted by the presence of the elderly doctor who never left his side and who fell asleep at dawn sitting up in a chair next to the bed. The little boy was so deeply impressed by the old man's devotion, he decided he wanted to do the same for other people when he grew up.

Dr. Piatt made the decision under very different circumstances.

"During World War II, I left my momma and daddy for *years*. I went straight from high school into service." He looked into my eyes as he said it, still visibly stunned by the enormous transition he'd been forced to make from Smoky Mountain farm boy to sailor in the Pacific.

"I was on the *Bunker Hill* and I was wounded." He stopped talking for a few moments, lost in the memory. Then he gathered himself and continued.

"Because of my experience in the war I wondered if there was any way I could ever make a doctor." He said it without emotion, but I knew the lack of detail in his story probably concealed terrible things he couldn't or didn't want to talk about.

After I spoke to him, I did some research. It turned out that even in the midst of a savage war, the aircraft carrier *Bunker Hill* had been a particularly hellish place to serve. Two Kamikaze planes bombed the carrier and then made suicide crashes into 100 fully-fueled airplanes that were parked on deck. A massive fire broke out from the bombings, crashes, and jet fuel.

Four hundred men perished in what some historians call the worst suicide attacks on Americans until the two planes crashed into the World Trade Center on 9/11.

A photographer on a nearby ship recorded images of the catastrophe. The archival photos display a shipboard inferno, the deck covered in a dense cloud of black smoke. This deadly smoke was then automatically, and catastrophically, pumped through the air intakes and asphyxiated the men trapped below.

Still, silent, black and white photographs could hardly convey what it must have been like to actually be there.

As I looked at the photos I wondered if the young sailor whose life had been so dramatically altered that day had ever realized that for fifty years he'd helped more people in a month than he'd seen die that day on the *Bunker Hill*.

"I'd have to get better to die."

Bird Island

Hearing this story was especially moving because I'd waited a bit too long before going to see Dr. Adams. He'd had a stroke before I arrived. His mind was fine, but his speech was impaired, so he never spoke a word during the first hour or so of the interview. He'd just smile or nod as his wife told me their favorite family stories. I maintained eye contact with him the whole time, just as if he was speaking, but it was actually his wife who did all the talking.

Then, when we were nearly finished, she mentioned he'd been a doctor in World War II. She tried to tell me where in the Pacific he'd been stationed, but she'd forgotten the name of the place.

When she paused to think, the doctor said, "Torishima."

We were both startled to hear him speak. He repeated in a calm and steady voice, "It was Torishima. That means *Bird Island*."

Then he told me this whole story himself in a clear voice.

"I was in my last year of medical school when World War II broke out. My class was told that because there was such a need for doctors, we'd be allowed to remain in school until we graduated and then we'd get a brief internship, but immediately after that we'd be inducted into the military.

"As soon as my internship was over I was sent to Japan. My battalion was billeted in an old city hall in Nago, Okinawa. A few hours after I arrived, in the middle of the night, the Japanese started bombing the building where we were sleeping. Everybody jumped up, grabbed their clothes, and ran. Well, everybody but me.

"I had no combat training. I was so shocked to be getting bombed almost immediately after arriving at the war, I was paralyzed with terror. I finally realized I needed to get out of the building. I left everything I owned inside and was the last one to leave. I got out just in the nick of time because the building was totally destroyed just after I cleared the front door. A piece of shrapnel hit me in the heel as I ran away. I was so embarrassed to be wounded under those circumstances I never applied for my purple heart.

"The next day they told me I was going to be transferred to an island where there was a signal corps. The island was called Torishima, which means *Bird Island* in Japanese. It was a volcanic rock in the middle of the ocean. There was nothing there. My job would be to watch for incoming airplanes and warn the Allies.

"I told them I needed to get some more clothes before I went anywhere, that I had only what I was standing up in. I was told not to worry about it. They promised I'd be on the island only for three or four days, and then they rushed me onto a transport.

"They dropped me and a few other men off on Torishima and left.

"Days, then weeks went by and no one came to get us. Eventually we realized the war had advanced to the point that nobody was going to come take us off that island for a good long while.

"I was stuck on Torishima from May to August, with one set of clothes.

"I was the battalion surgeon on the island, which made me the officer in charge. I knew nothing about being in the military, but I figured I better keep the morale up, so I started publishing a little newspaper.

"I had a shortwave radio where I got the news each day. Then I'd type it up and make six copies with the carbon paper we had in our supplies and post them at different places around the island. The news was very popular. If I was late, soldiers would come to my tent asking for it.

"There were a few coconut trees on the island. None of us could climb them, so we'd throw rocks to knock the coconuts down. I was the best rock thrower on the island. I was proud of this skill because it was pretty much the only useful one I had, aside from writing the newspaper.

"The island was very small, especially at high tide. In fact, it was so small, one night when a Japanese sub overheard a radio broadcast coming from us, they torpedoed us. They torpedoed an *island* because it was so little, they thought it was a ship or another submarine!

"It was a tiny place, but not so small that a *torpedo* could hurt anybody.

"But the torpedo incident served to remind us that there was a fierce war going on all around us. There was a master sergeant with us who'd seen a lot of combat. He was from Texas and could do anything. Nothing scared him. I, of course, had seen almost no combat, could do very little, and was scared of pretty much everything. I told him he'd have to be in charge while we were marooned on the island or we'd all end up dead. That was, of course, strictly against military rules. I had to beg him to take over, and we all swore secrecy about what we were doing, but, thank goodness, he finally agreed.

"It was pretty boring being stuck out there on a rock in the middle of the Pacific Ocean. So, to have something to do, we decided to make some rafts. The sergeant figured out how to make a floating platform from empty gas tanks and we'd go out swimming and fishing on them.

"A captain from New York and I were out on a raft one day and a wave overturned it. The captain managed to keep hold of the raft, but I got thrown out into the water and got my clothes knocked off. I had to swim to shore. The men teased me a lot about that. They'd say the officer was supposed to stay with his ship! All I could think about was where would I ever find some more clothes!

"We were eventually picked up, the war finally ended, and I was sent back to Japan with the army of occupation. I was nervous about this. I didn't know how the Japanese people would react to us. But the emperor told them they'd lost and they accepted it. Then they were as nice as they could be. I made friends and stayed in contact with several of them for many years.

"A rich family in Yokohama moved into the basement of their own house and let me live in the best part. I was made the venereal disease control officer. There was legalized prostitution in Japan at that time and I was put in charge of examining the prostitutes every Friday. I did that for over a year, then I got to go back home."

As soon as he said the word *home* Dr. Adams stopped speaking. He never spoke again for the rest of my visit.

"I got corporal tunnel syndrome."

Uncle Eli

Medicinal herbs are often scraggly or even stinky and repulsive looking plants that unsuspecting people would judge to be nothing more than noxious weeds. And because when they're not blooming they don't look like much, a lot of wildflowers are considered to be weeds, too.

But if you know what's what, you can look at a fungus and see a life saving medicine. And if you're there at the right time, you can see an ugly brown stick sprout a delicate flower.

In the same vein, it's no secret that some of the best *docs* aren't officially certified doctors at all. Mothers, for example. Here's a story about a man who wasn't technically a doctor, but who was willing to try to help out—just on an interim basis during an emergency.

"I come from a family of pharmacists," said Dr. Hendricks. "Most of my childhood I assumed I'd be a pharmacist when I grew up, but then something happened to my Uncle Eli and it inspired me to go to medical school instead.

"Uncle Eli was visiting a coal mining camp, helping the local doctor get his small dispensary in order, when the doctor suddenly and unexpectedly died.

"This was in a very isolated area where the only way to get there was to drive up a creek bed in a car with a high ground clearance. Anything large, like furniture, had to be brought in on a railroad car.

"With the local doctor dead, there was no other doctor or hospital the people could reach in a reasonable amount of time.

"The mining company asked Uncle Eli to stay on, just until they could find a replacement, and he reluctantly agreed. He knew some first aid and was willing to do what he could for the miners and their families—temporarily, on an emergency basis.

"There was no drugstore, so he dispensed all his own medicines.

"He bought aspirin made up in three different colors—green, pink, and white. They were manufactured for placebos by a pharmacy. He'd say, 'Did them green pills hep ye? No? Then try some of these red'ns.'

"And if none of the pills worked, he'd give them one of the two liquids he kept. They were both mild sedatives. He'd prescribe either elixir of phenobarbital which was pink, or elixir of butisol which was green. If one didn't work, he'd switch the patient over to the other.

"He'd have to remember what color he'd given out for particular ailments and be sure not to give the same color for a different ailment. People would have lost confidence in him if he'd given them all the same thing.

"His other comprehensive remedy was *blue mass,* a laxative

that was given for everything in the coal camp.

"Of course some people would insist on a shot. They believed they couldn't get well with a pill or a liquid medicine. If they asked for a shot, he learned over time he might as well go ahead and give them one or they'd be back because they wouldn't get well from medicine they didn't believe in.

"Uncle Eli knew one of the great secrets of healing—patients needed hope. If they had hope, they could recover from nearly anything. He was a master healer even though he didn't have much real medical know-how because he loved and understood people. He was willing to take the burdens of total strangers onto himself and try to help lighten them with whatever he had on hand.

"They never did find a replacement doctor willing to come live in such a poor, isolated place. So Uncle Eli ended up staying there for thirty years.

"Eventually, when he was an old man, he was awarded a retroactive M.D. by the state legislature. They figured he'd earned it."

"I might be one of them that's not gettin the real pills. What do you think Doc, could I be takin a gazebo and not know it?"

Hopeth All Things

A lot of the heroism of doctoring comes during lonely, desperate hours of waiting. I was struck by how many of the doctors had stories of helpless, nearly hopeless situations where they sat with a person who might not make it.

"I attended the birth of a child at home for a family of Jehovah's Witnesses," said Dr. Clifton. The mother delivered in the middle of the night and she hemorrhaged.

"Jehovah's witnesses don't believe in blood transfusions. The mother didn't want to take any blood. It was against her religion.

"The family agreed with her and insisted that no matter what happened, even if she was going to die without it, she couldn't have any blood.

"Let me tell you, that's a bad feeling, a helpless feeling.

"You are mighty lonesome when you're by yourself with somebody who's bleeding and they won't take any blood. All I could do was give her Pitocin and glucose and wait. I stayed up with her all night, worried I was watching a young woman, the mother of a newborn, slowly bleed to death.

"Finally, at dawn, she stopped bleeding. It was a close thing, but she managed to survive."

"One night at the Emergency Room I looked up and a young Black woman, just a girl, was walking down the hall pouring blood like a fire hose. I'd never seen anything like it. She was covering the whole floor with her blood.

"She had placenta previa. That's when the placenta is not anchored properly. It rests over the opening of the cervix. It's really dangerous.

"I had a good RN working with me that night. We threw the girl up on the table, I put on an extra-long surgical glove, and reached in and got hold of that placenta and pulled it out.

"She quit bleeding. She'd have died in another couple of minutes. Her hematocrit was 9. The normal level for a woman is 35.

"There was no blood left in her. She'd lost nearly every drop of blood in her body. We filled her up with saline to keep her blood pressure up. Then we gave her a transfusion.

"She lived and did fine. She came from strong and tough people, thank goodness.

"They'd refused to take her in any of the hospitals in the area, because she was Black.

"I moved away after that. I didn't want to stay in an area where things like that went on."

"If World War II didn't kill him, that Jap doctor won't be able to git him either."

— said by an elderly veteran's wife after he'd been taken to the Emergency Room having a heart attack and the family discovered the cardiologist was of Japanese ancestry.

Dead Man in the Dining Room

Being the child of a country doctor isn't easy. From a very young age you get confronted with situations that most grownups would be hard-pressed to cope with.

An example of this was the day my brother David and I, I was ten and he was eight, came home from school and found a dead man in the dining room.

We came in the side door of the house which opened into the dining room. You had to go through the dining room to get to any other room in the house because we didn't have keys to any other door.

As I came in I glanced to the right toward the dining table and was horrified to see a man lying on a cot just on the other side of the dining table. He was totally still and silent. He was also Black.

He was stretched out flat in front of a large picture window. But he didn't look like he was in any condition to be enjoying the view.

David came in just behind me and saw him, too. We both screamed and ran back outside. We didn't know what to do. We were supposed to go inside and wait until Momma and Daddy got home, but who wanted to go inside and wait with a dead body?

It was a real problem. We'd have to get past the body and into the kitchen to reach the nearest telephone to call Momma and ask her what to do. We were raised over the telephone, so this was a common problem—how to get to phones and who should get to talk first whenever we had fights, or crises, or were just bored.

We decided that sooner or later we'd have to go inside to call for help. We knew if we could just reach our parents they'd fix the situation.

Moving close together for courage, we crept back into the dining room, sneaking by the inert man. And then we bolted into the kitchen and by unspoken agreement kept going all the way to the far end of the house to the telephone farthest away from the body.

We dialed Momma and said at the same time, "Momma! There's a dead man in the dining room!"

"What?" she asked obviously distracted by something else.

"Please, you gotta come home right now. There's somebody dead in the dining room. Get him out of here!"

Both of us were babbling urgently into the phone in rough whispers and begging as fast as we could talk.

"There's no dead man in the dining room," Momma assured us, "I don't know what you're talking about. Calm down and go watch TV."

"We can't. He's just on the other side of the dining room table!"

Unable to get us to listen to her, she passed the phone to my father. In tones of absolute authority he said, "Carolyn, go in there and look for an IV bottle on a stand next to the cot."

"Oh no Daddy. I can't go back in there."

"Carolyn, do what I'm telling you. Go look and come back and tell me if you see an IV bottle with a tube going down into that man's arm. Do it now!"

I handed the phone to my little brother and crept down the hall toward the dining room. David stayed on the phone in case something awful happened to me.

Sure enough, as I peeked around the corner of the kitchen into the dining room, I could see there was a bottle hanging on a metal stand next to the cot and a clear plastic tube running from it to the man's arm.

I ran back and said, "Yes, there's a tube! I saw it!"

I didn't really know why this was important though until Daddy shouted into the phone, "Do you think I'd waste an IV on a dead man? Those things are not cheap!"

I reluctantly began to see the possibility that the man might not be dead, but still wasn't convinced.

"He's not moving or breathing or anything. I think he's dead."

"Carolyn, that's Milton!" Milton was an unemployed alcoholic who Daddy gave a job cleaning the office at night. Many times he had nowhere to live and stayed in the basement of the office.

"Milton's really sick. He needs us to help him. He can't afford to go to the hospital, so I'm gonna take care of him at home. Leave the man alone. Okay? He needs to rest!" He slammed down the phone, too busy to continue with such a silly discussion.

David and I were embarrassed to have made such a mistake, but still too scared to come out of the back bedroom until Momma and Daddy came home several hours later.

Milton eventually got better. Then a couple of nights later we were rewarded for our humanitarian efforts by having a cross burned in our yard.

For years, my brother and I were oblivious to the significance of this fire in our front yard because Momma and Daddy lied and told us it was for a celebration, like the 4th of July.

"I saw a kid who had second degree burns on his butt.

"I asked him how he got them.

"He said he was putting gas in his car and some of it splashed on his pants. He tried to dry the damp patch by holding a cigarette lighter next to it."

Like a House Afire

Anybody who grew up in the Smokies knows when you make a loud noise in a valley, or holler in a hollow, the sound bounces and rolls against the sides of the steep ridges, so by the time you hear it, you can't be certain where it originated from.

This story is about a young doctor, new to the area, who experienced a similar problem over the telephone. The Smokies is one of the few places where the phrase *where there's smoke, there's fire* is generally not true. But sometimes it is, as Dr. DeHaven learned.

"I hadn't been a doctor but two or three months when I got a call I answered myself because it was after-hours. A panicked little girl's voice said, 'Doctor come quick! My brothers and sisters are asleep!' Then she hung up without telling me who or where she was.

"I was shocked. All I could do was wait next to the phone, hoping she'd call back.

"Two minutes later the phone rang again. It was the same little girl. This time she said, 'Doctor, doctor, come quick! There's smoke in the house and I can't wake any of 'em up!'

"'Honey, where are you?' I asked.

"'You gotta come,' she said. 'They're too heavy!' Then she hung up again.

"It was awful. I stood by the phone, totally helpless, and prayed as I waited for another call. When the phone rang a third time, I snatched it up and said as fast as I could, 'Don't hang up! I don't know where you are. I'll come help you, but don't hang up! Tell me where you are!'

"'I'm Annie,' she said. 'My grandma's Wilma Shanks.'

"I recognized the name. I'd met the child's mother. She'd come to see me out of curiosity when I'd first come to town. She hadn't been sick. People used to do that. They'd come by to see what sort of person you were.

"I still didn't have any idea where the child was, but now I at least had something to go on, so I called the fire chief because I knew he'd lived in the area all his life and he might recognize the name.

"The chief knew where the family lived. He said he'd come pick me up right away and take me there. I expected him to arrive in a fire truck, but he didn't. He had more presence of mind than I did. He ran down to the funeral home and ask to borrow a hearse because there were no ambulances back then.

"Hearses were the only vehicles you could use to transport people who were lying down. The funeral director said he'd drive, so the fire chief, a mortician, and I all piled into the hearse and took off for Owl Valley.

"When we got to the house it was boiling with smoke. The little girl, who it turned out was just five years old, had somehow managed to drag all of her siblings out onto the front porch. She had her four brothers and sisters, from six to fourteen years old, lying there in a row, unconscious, each with the bright cherry pink faces that indicate carbon monoxide poisoning.

"A pan of green beans was on fire on the stove and every person in the house had succumbed to the carbon monoxide except for the little girl. Somehow, maybe because she was so short and closest to the floor, and maybe because she kept running in and out of the smoke, she stayed alert enough to help the rest of them.

"After they were given oxygen, they all revived and were fine. The littlest child had managed to save all the other kids. It was a miracle."

The doctor touched his abundant head of pure white hair and said, "I'm pretty sure those first two phone calls were what started my hair going gray."

"I don't have no trouble breathin.
I'm as long-winded as I ever was."

Hazardous Housecall

The variety of frustrations that doctors face when making rural housecalls is astounding: getting lost or stuck, being harried by livestock, pets, or angry relatives. But some housecalls get even more dangerous.

Tennessee is nicknamed "The Volunteer State" because it consistently contributes a high percentage of volunteers to the military. It's a fact that soldiers from the Smokies are more likely to be wounded or killed in battle than soldiers from any other state. And an extremely high percentage of military snipers come from this same area, probably because guns play such a significant role in the local cultural life and children are trained to use them from a very young age.

This love of firearms and proficiency with them means doctors in the Smokies can get into some unique situations. Dr. Lacey, one of the doctors who had multiple board certifications and yet still chose to work in a rural area in family medicine, told me this story when I asked him about the scariest situation he ever got into.

"I got a phone call from a woman asking me to come out to a house about five miles from my office. She said the sheriff was already on his way, then she hung up.

"Well, I didn't know what the problem was, but it couldn't be anything normal or pleasant if the sheriff had been called. So I took my time. I knew the sheriff well and I knew he wasn't going to be knocking himself out to get over there quickly, so I did everything I could think of before heading out. I rearranged the papers on my desk, tidied up the office, inventoried and repacked my bag, and then drove over there real slow.

"I still got there before the sheriff.

"Before I'd even gotten out of the car I could hear shouting coming from inside the house. I got my bag, climbed up on the porch, and knocked on the front door.

"Nobody answered, so I went on inside. There was a big row going on in the kitchen.

"I peeked around the corner to see if I could figure out why they'd called me, but I couldn't make head nor tails of it. They all appeared pretty vigorous to me. It looked like a four way fight between a husband and wife and their daughter and her husband.

"The four of them were bunched together, scuffling in the corner of the room. They were flinging each other all over the counters, flailing and cussing. Then the mother slipped and fell. But the others were too carried away to notice that they were trampling her. I heard a crack like a rifle shot and the mother shouted, 'Now you've done it! You've gone and broke my leg! Where's my pocketbook! I'm gettin my pistol!'

"When she scrabbled her way out from under the rest of them, I decided it was time for me to leave. I didn't know if they'd even noticed me, but I played it safe and crawled off real quiet through the living room, staying low. Then I slipped out the front door and ran and jumped in my car. The sheriff still hadn't arrived, so I took off.

"About half way back to the office, I realized I'd left my bag and hat in the living room!

"Well, when I walked in the door of my office the phone was ringing. It was the same family again. They wanted me to come back and look at the momma's leg.

"I told them there was no way I'd come back to that house, but I'd be willing to meet them at the hospital and take a look at her leg there, on two conditions: First, they had to promise they'd bring my hat and bag to the hospital with them. Second, they had to swear they'd leave the guns at home.

"They agreed. This time I *really* took my time before leaving the office. But they were as good as their word. They brought my hat and bag to the emergency room. And sure enough, the momma'd broken her leg, so I set it.

"The sheriff never showed up and I never did find out what the first call was for."

"Your hands are shakin so bad, you could thread a sewin machine and it a runnin!"

— one patient to another in the waiting room.

Red Light

"There were several wrecks at the red light near my office," said Dr. Thompson.

"One day I heard someone shouting, 'Man's had a wreck!'

"It was a guy on a motorcycle, who'd been hit by car. He was knocked into the yard of the house next door.

"His right leg was broken, and twisted around so that his right foot was up even with his hip!

"In those days the ambulances were provided by funeral homes, there was no Rural Metro. Some of the 'ambulances' were black, some were other colors, but they always had a chenille bedspread with them, and they weren't trained emergency medical technicians.

"Roger's Funeral Home sent a car to this wreck and these two fellows came down to the scene of the accident with a stretcher and a big blue blanket that had a big 'R' embroidered on it.

"I said, 'Be careful loading him up, or he'll go into shock.'

"They said, 'Let's get this leg straightened out,' and reached for the man's ankle.

"I shouted, 'Don't you dare!'

"It gives me chills to think of what those two did in the name of first aid."

"Just a few months later a man came running into the office shouting, 'A feller out here's been shot! He needs help!'

"I grabbed up my stethoscope and ran outside with it. First, I saw a car sitting crooked in the middle of the street with the driver's door open. Then I saw there was a man leaning against the wall of the pizza place a couple of doors down, holding his belly, bleeding.

"I felt like a fool standing on the sidewalk holding a stethoscope. What could I do with that? I ran back inside and grabbed up a pile of four by four cotton swabs and a roll of adhesive tape. What were you supposed to grab at a time like that? I didn't know!

"I ran back out with this new equipment and pressed the wad of cotton squares against the man's abdomen and shouted at my receptionist to call the police and an ambulance.

"Just moments after the receptionist had gone in to make the calls, a man jumped out of the passenger side of the car and ran in the door of my office carrying a pistol!

"*Hell*, I thought. I can't leave my receptionist alone in there to face a man with a gun. I better go help her.

"So, I handed the injured man the roll of tape and took off back to my office. But before I got to the door, the second man came back outside, this time without the gun. He was holding his arm, which was bleeding profusely.

"He sat down on my front steps and fainted.

"What was I supposed to do now?

"I made sure my receptionist was okay. She said the guy had only come as far as the waiting room and then turned around and gone back outside.

"The first responder to the scene was not the police or the ambulance but the TV news! The second bunch who got there were in a big red fire truck. The police were third, and then last, very late, was the ambulance. The ambulance attendants tried to go for the arm wound first, but I made them deal with the gut shot instead.

"We got the two injured men loaded up and carted off in the ambulance and I told the police about one of them going into my office with a gun and coming out without it. They went inside to search and found where he'd jammed his pistol down in a magazine rack to hide it. They showed me the gun. It had target grips and nickel plating. It was nice. I wish I'd kept my mouth shut. If I had, I'd have gotten to keep it.

"I was going to call my son to bring the garden hose so we could wash off the sidewalk and steps, but the firemen said they'd do it. They hooked up their hose, sprayed up and down the street, and got rid of all the blood.

"The TV truck was the last to leave. I couldn't figure out why they kept hanging around, but then a pretty lady journalist fixed her makeup and hair and at 6:00 they turned a camera on her and she broadcasted a report from the sidewalk, even though everybody was long gone.

"The story made the 6:00 news.

"My wife saw it and told me what had happened. It turned out that the two fellows had been riding in the car together and the passenger was fiddling with his gun and it went off. He accidentally shot himself through the arm and the same bullet got the driver in the belly."

"It's either feast or phantom."

Eyes Wide Shut

"I had a patient who fainted at *everything*," said Dr. James. No matter what we did, he fainted. You had to brace yourself whenever you entered the room, because you knew he was going to keel over. Some people are just fainters. They can't help it. And it's not just patients.

"I had an emergency where a man came in with a terrible laceration that was too much for one person to handle, so I asked my nurse to run up the street a few doors to get the dentist to come help me.

"He came to the office, took one look at the guy on the table, and fainted dead into the floor. My nurse dragged him out of the way so she could help me herself. The two of us managed to keep the patient from bleeding to death. But we had to do it without any assistance from the dentist. He laid there in the floor, unconscious, during the entire surgery.

"People are funny about pain, too. Some people are so tough they don't need any anesthetic or pain pills. Others, will scream before you even touch 'em. I had fellow who shouted when he saw I had a syringe in my hand.

"I'm just going to give you a shot," I said.

"'*Why?*' he hollered. 'I'm *already* hurt!'

Another guy said, 'Do whatever you gotta do, Doc. I can take the pain. There's no need for anesthetic.'

"Then he screamed when I barely touched him, *twice.*

"When I lived near Harlan, one night a drunk walked up the mountain to our cabin and knocked on the door. When my wife went to answer it, she found a man covered in blood standing on the front porch. She called for me to come quick.

"There was a bench on the porch and I had the fellow sit on it. He was cut horribly and was losing a lot of blood.

"I asked him what had happened and he told me he'd been in a fight.

"The other fellow had an axe.

"The cuts were terrible, some went all the way to the bone. I have no idea how the man was able to make his way to my house for help.

"He sat on that bench and didn't make a sound while I put 158 stitches in him. And he recovered without getting any infection at all."

"I know I weigh 360 because I can get on a 350 scale and hang onto the wall and the needle will jiggle. My wife's so big we have to go to the coal yard to weigh her."

Emergency Medicine

The Smokies are justifiably famous for their infinitely variable cloudscapes. My favorite is when there's a low-lying blanket of clouds and the highest peaks rise like disconnected islands out of a turbulent sea of white.

Once I was standing at Newfound Gap enjoying a peaceful sunset when a cloud drifted through a stand of dead trees nearby. Suddenly the white mists were stained a hellish orange that transformed the world into an apocalyptic landscape filled with fire and brimstone. It was terrifying and awe-inspiring.

Some days are just like that. They start out fine, but then things change.

My favorite pharmacist told me a story about a situation like that. I probably wasn't as sympathetic as I should've been because there's nothing more entertaining than hearing about a medical professional encountering the health care system as a patient. They can dish it out, but are notoriously reluctant to take it. In this case, my friend Frank DeCoville had an unforgettable run-in with emergency services.

When I worked as Daddy's receptionist, it was part of my job to phone the local pharmacist, Frank, several times a day to give him the details on prescriptions. Frank was a major character. He was Daddy's counterpart in that he also provided a full range of services for all the local down-and-outs, the crazy, the societal misfits, and rejects. He got them groceries, made sure their lawns were mowed, helped them fill out their insurance and disability papers, and he did this, like Daddy did, out of his own pocket and on his own time.

One day I called to give him a prescription for some non-narcotic pain relievers for Estole Chesney, the community malingerer, and to tell him Estole had announced an intention to *go for a check*. A drug addict for many years, Estole had now decided to seek a declaration of disability from the State of Tennessee, claiming an inability to work on account of a *bad back*. He wanted Daddy to shore up his claim, but Daddy wouldn't do it.

I told Frank about Daddy's theory that most of the truly disabled people were in no position to negotiate the complicated state bureaucracy, so only con artists had what it took to game the system persuasively and persistently enough to get declared disabled.

"He's right. Estole will probably get disability," Frank said, exasperated. "You know I broke my back years ago and it still hurts when I've been standing for a long time, but I'd never be able to get a dime from the state! I'm lucky if I get time to take an aspirin."

"I didn't know you'd broken your back," I said. "What happened?"

"Oh, I was duck hunting, by myself, which was stupid. I was walking down this dirt road beside a marsh and a bunch of ducks flew right over my head. I couldn't believe my luck. I hopped up on an old dock and started blasting away. Unfortunately the wood was rotted and broke under me and I fell through.

"Actually I fell only half way through. I had hold of my shotgun and landed with it crossways, so it kept me from falling farther than my chest. But I was stuck, half of me above and half below the dock, with my feet dangling in cold water."

"Oh Frank!" I said.

"I was in terrible pain, too. I knew I'd done something to myself so I waited, hoping somebody would come along, but there was nobody around. Nobody even knew where I was! My feet and then legs went numb. I thought it was from the cold water and figured I better get out of it.

"I had to kick and squirm for I don't know how long 'til I got myself loose. I finally crawled up onto the dock and then the road, but I hurt so bad there was no way could I stand up. I laid in the road awhile, but nobody came, so I had to drag myself back to my pickup using the shotgun to pull myself along.

"It took *forever* to get there. I laid beside the truck for a long time 'til I decided I was gonna have to haul my own self up into it somehow. I was able to do it, barely, but it about killed me. I managed to drive myself to the little hospital near Tellico using the shotgun to mash the gas and brake with. I had to use the gun because I couldn't feel my feet!"

"Oh goodness, Frank, that's awful!"

"Oh honey, it's not over yet. I somehow manage to drive using the gun, and I manage to find a hospital and even locate the emergency entrance and drive right up to the doors, but does anybody come out to help me? No! I blew the horn and waited. Nothing.

"Finally, and I'm really mad by now, I get out of the truck and start trying to walk in, using the shotgun for a cane, and this nurse sticks her head out of the ER door and hollers, 'Listen Buddy, you can't come in here with that!'

"I hollered back, 'Well I certainly can't come in without it!'"

I laughed until tears streamed down my face.

Frank said, "I'd broken my back and my left leg below the knee. I have to stand up all day at work and it hurts. Do you think the state will send me a check every month?"

"Not unless you use the same cane in your disability hearing you used at the emergency room."

As I hung up the phone I marveled at a world where a guy like Frank who year in and year out helped hundreds of people for no reason whatsoever except that he had a kind heart, when he was in desperate need, he couldn't get help from anybody, even a nurse at a hospital emergency room. It figures.

"I got walkin ammonia."

Deliverance

The ubiquitous fogs and mists for which the Smokies are named are, in part, due to a super-abundance of moisture in the area. This wealth of moisture produces many boisterous creeks and rivers. The great rivers, in turn, provided an excuse for the creation of the areas most deeply mixed blessing—TVA.

I was thinking about this as I drove to see Dr. Whitfield, so I took a little detour to look at the Tellico Dam, the last gasp in TVA's dam-building frenzy. Little did I know this dam was to feature large in one of the stories he was going to tell me.

The story is not only one of the funniest stories I've ever heard in my life, but it's also an absolutely true comic parallel to *Deliverance*. It's also a far more realistic portrait of southern men and the shenanigans they get up to than James Dickey's dark fictional tale.

"A patient came in with a cut on his head and complaining of a sore neck. He was bruised all over, but especially on his back and buttocks. I asked him what he'd gotten into and he told me he'd had an accident while floating the *Little T*, a nickname for the Little Tennessee River.

"There was something in his manner that implied there was more of a story than he was letting on, and sure enough, while I sewed his head up, he admitted what really happened.

"The Little T runs through some of the most beautiful valleys in the country. The local people were terribly upset that TVA's Tellico Dam, when it was finished, was going to flood hundreds of family farms and submerge a lot of gorgeous scenery under yet another reservoir. There was a long and bitter battle between horribly mismatched opponents. At the end it was pitiful. Elderly women barricaded themselves with shotguns inside the old home-places where they'd been born and lived in all their lives and refused to leave, but the government removed them by force.

"Anyway, before the construction on the dam was completed, floating the Little T one last time was the big thing to do for the men who lived in the area. Judges, lawyers, doctors, would hire a ranger to take them down the river and they'd fish. Then they'd camp out. The ranger'd fry up the fish and the men would eat 'em.

"In the communities near the area that was going to be flooded, all the men were talking about making one last trip down the river.

"My patient was new to the area and had kept hoping some of the local men would invite him to go with them, but they never did. Finally, at the last minute, he decided if he didn't go now he was going to miss his chance to do it altogether, so he decided he'd go alone.

He picked a Sunday morning for his expedition. He didn't have the money to hire a professional guide or a boat and he didn't have a boat of his own, but the judge offered to let him borrow a canoe.

"He knew nothing whatsoever about canoes, but he borrowed it anyway, because he was desperate to fit in with the local men, to be cool. He put the canoe in the back of his pickup truck and drove over to the Ocoee, a powerful tributary that he figured would take him quickly out to the Little T.

"To give you an idea of what kind of location he'd decided to put in, the Ocoee is where the whitewater kayaking competition was held for the 1996 Olympics.

"It's an understatement to say this was a poor place for a novice to learn to paddle a canoe, but he was a big man, 250 pounds, most of it above the waist, so he figured he could handle it. He got the canoe out of the back of his truck and set it into the foaming, spewing Ocoee. He was strong enough to keep hold of the boat, but he couldn't figure out how to get into it in a raging torrent. It was like trying to hop onto a bucking horse from a standing start. He tried all sorts of approaches, but none of them worked.

"Finally he hurled himself into the pointy end, but that made the canoe tilt straight up into the air where it remained poised for just a second until it flipped over and hit him in the head, knocking him loopy. Being clubbed on the head loosened his grip for just a second and the boat shot off into the whitewater without him. It was very soon gone from sight.

"This panicked him. He dared not lose the judge's canoe.

"He ran back to his pickup and gave chase, racing down a gravel road that ran alongside the river. In a couple of minutes, he caught sight of the canoe. He was so determined not to let it out of his sight again, he ran a stop sign at the first intersection and T-boned another car.

"His truck would still run, so as quickly as he could, he exchanged insurance information with the fellow he hit and raced away, trying to catch up with the canoe again, but it was too late. After a couple of miles he hadn't managed to regain sight of the canoe, and the road veered away from the river.

"He needed a new plan.

"He got an idea about how to get out into the river to recover the canoe. He went to K-Mart and bought a child's soft bottom wading pool. He wanted to make sure the pool didn't have any holes in it before the left the store parking lot, so he had to blow it up by mouth.

"Hurriedly blowing up a wading pool by mouth in addition to his head injury, sore neck from a car wreck, and panic over losing the judge's canoe made him nearly faint with frustration, pain, and rage, but he forced himself to focus and stay on task.

"Then, made a little more cautious by recent events, he raced over to a friend's house to test his watercraft in a swimming pool before trying to ride it through whitewater. It worked. The wading pool held his weight and remained afloat without swamping. He took it back to the river access, flung himself into it, and shot out into the rapids.

"His watercraft stayed afloat there too, but his butt took a terrible beating against the notoriously rocky river bottom. He found the ride less painful if he splayed himself out like Garfield, keeping the draft of his wading pool as shallow as possible

"Soon after he passed the last place he remembered seeing the canoe, he ran into a fog bank over the river that was typical in the area. In a few minutes the fog got so thick he could barely see his hand in front of his face. Floating blind, he ran aground on an island in the middle of the river and was stranded. There was nothing he could do but sit and wait.

"A couple of hours later the fog lifted and, as it did, he spied the judge's canoe which had also run aground nearby. He dog paddled his wading pool over to the canoe and rigged a rope to tow it. He knew better than to try to get into it again.

"He needed both hands to paddle his wading pool, so he held the canoe tow rope with his teeth the whole time it took him to float to a launching ramp two miles downriver. Exhausted and battered, he staggered onto dry land at last and tried to hitch a ride back to his truck, but he'd drifted so far downriver, the men at the landing didn't know him.

"They figured he was either drunk or crazy to come floating up in a child's pool splayed out like Garfield, bleeding from the head, and towing a canoe by way of a rope in his mouth. Nobody wanted to have anything to do with him, so he was forced to pay for transportation for himself and his two watercraft back to his wrecked truck so he could take the canoe back to the judge and himself to the doctor.

"He never did get to float, fish, or camp out on the Little T. TVA flooded the valley before he could recuperate and mount another expedition.

"His wife was not sympathetic. She said every single thing that happened to him that day served him right for missing church."

A tractor trailer whizzed by me on the interstate and made several very aggressive lane changes as it went out of sight. There was a sign on the back of the truck.

"If you see any dangerous moves by this vehicle please call . . ."

The telephone number had been covered over by a piece of duct tape.

Going to the Dogs

There's a stereotype about rural physicians treating some of their patients for free. What's not as widely known is that country doctors often end up giving these same patients whatever cash they have in their pockets, too.

Dr. Carlton, a quiet, gentle man who lived near where I grew up was a notoriously soft touch. He would never confess something like this himself, but his son told me he made a housecall every day for weeks on a young girl who was terribly sick with rheumatic fever. Her family was poor, so he never charged them anything for his visits. And every morning, right after he saw the child, he slipped a dollar bill underneath her pillow so the family would have enough money to buy food.

If he was seeing one of these sorts of patients in his office things got trickier. His bookkeeper complained whenever she caught him working for free, but she would've killed him if she'd realized he was giving away cash as well! So he had to be sneaky. He'd write out a prescription and fold it in half, then wait until her back was turned so he could stuff it with enough paper money to pay for the medicine and hand it to the patient with her none the wiser.

There's another stereotype about country doctors being willing to treat animals occasionally. That's true too, as Dr. Wilson confessed.

"For years we didn't have a hospital anywhere near here. People had to be driven a long way to a city to be hospitalized. I finally got a little hospital built here but it turned out to be a mixed blessing, for me anyway. It meant I had to put in a full day at my office and then work half the night or more manning the emergency room.

"I was working late one night and was just worn out. I was in an awful mood. Then right outside the emergency room door, an enormous dogfight got going.

"A nurse headed out to try to break it up and shoo the dogs away. When she went out through the automatic doors, a little cur dog ran in on three legs. Nobody could catch the little thing. He ran into the back and down the hall and disappeared

"This was just about the last straw from my point of view. I went after the dog, but couldn't see him anywhere. I worked my way down the hall, looking in every room with an open door. I searched all the way to the back of the hospital where the radiology department was. In radiology there were three small curtained cubicles where people undressed and put on gowns before getting x-rayed. I opened the curtains to one of these cubicles and there was the little dog sitting on a stool, just like a person would.

"I was so tired I didn't have the energy left to see even one more patient, much less a dog. And this poor creature was so thin and dirty, it was obviously just a stray.

"Just what I needed.

"I stood and stared at him, but the little dog didn't run away. He just sat there calmly, looking at me, waiting for me to help him. He was obviously hurt. He was bleeding from a bad bite on one of his hind legs.

"The way he was sitting there on the stool like he was waiting to be x-rayed, I didn't have the heart to throw him out. I examined him and could feel the fracture in his leg. I don't know how he knew where to come for help, but I decided he deserved to be x-rayed since he'd come to the right place.

"He was extremely gentle, even though he had to be in a lot of pain. He seemed to understand what was happening. I believed I could set what turned out to be three fractures in his back leg, so I did the best I could, then took another x-ray to make sure I had the bones correctly positioned. The leg looked perfect, so I put his leg in a little cast.

"I took him home with me after work, intending to keep him just for the night. The next day we posted notices about a lost dog, but nobody ever claimed him. So I kept him and he was a great friend to me for many years. I named him Jake. He was the smartest dog I ever had.

"Part of my brain tells me it was just an accident that he ran into the x-ray cubicle the night he got his leg broken. But another part of me says he knew just what he was doing.

"I always try to remember Jake whenever I'm tired and

asked if I'd be willing to see another patient. Jake taught me that with just a few minutes of kindness you can earn a friend for life. That's an important lesson."

I asked a blind friend why she didn't use a guide dog. She said she'd tried and they were great, but having the dog caused problems that never would've occurred to her.

"I was out practicing with my dog downtown and got lost, so I asked a person standing next to me on a street corner for directions. The fellow I asked got down on his *knees* and gave detailed directions to the dog!

"Then he stood up and whispered to me, 'These guide dogs are really incredible, aren't they?'

"After that I decided to use a cane."

"The heart doctor said my heart sounds like a skreakin door."

Appointment to Get Hurt

I watched Daddy finish writing up the results of the rigorous physical zinc miners were required to have if they worked on mine rescue teams. This particular physical was on a good friend of the family, Matthew DeCoville.

All the miners were given nicknames by the other miners that they were known by when they were underground. Co-workers might not even know each other's real names. Matthew's nickname was *Rambo, King of the G.I. Joes*. He was a stunning physical specimen who was famous in the community for his strength and agility.

"Well, Matt," Daddy said, "Everything looks good. You're still in great shape."

Matthew frowned. "I don't know Doc. I'm gettin old. I turn forty-five next week."

"Goodness, Matt, that's not old. I'm seventy. That's *old*."

Matthew didn't look convinced though. "Well," he said, "I

figure I better go ahead and do whatever I might wanna do, before I can't do it anymore."

"Like what?" I asked.

"Oh, like bull riding."

"Lord, Matthew," I blurted out. "*Please* don't do that."

But it was too late. Apparently he'd already mentioned this same concern at work—that he wanted to try one last physical feat before he got too feeble—and a bunch of the miners had gotten together and paid his entry fee for the amateur bull riding event in an upcoming rodeo.

Daddy, his nurse Alma, and I were shocked that he'd do something so foolish. It was bad enough that he did dangerous things at work, but it made no sense at all to do them in his spare time, too.

A few days later, when a nineteen year old professional bull rider came in with a cold, I told him what Matthew was going to do and asked him what he thought would happen. He shook his head mournfully.

"These old guys," he said, "when they try to ride, they break bones. Their bones just snap like kindling when they hit the ground. Arms, legs, collar bones—they just snap like little sticks when they hit that dirt. He's gonna get hurt *real* bad."

I winced.

The boy looked at me, eyes serious beneath the brim of his black cowboy hat, "Ma'am, you better stop him."

I knew my limitations, though. No power on earth could stop Matthew when he set his mind on something. That's how he'd gotten the nickname *Rambo, King of the G.I. Joes*. I worried that he was falling for his own publicity.

It felt odd to sit around waiting for Matthew's bull ride. Even Daddy commented on it. In four decades he'd never made a single appointment and he'd never had to wait for a planned injury to occur.

Then, right on schedule, the day after his ride, Matthew came in. He was wearing a short-sleeved shirt, displaying a collage of hideous bruises on his right arm.

"You're hurt!" I accused, and reached to touch the discolorations.

He flinched when I touched him and said, "I'd like to say it looks worse than it feels, but it's really the other way around."

He explained that the injured arm was the one he'd used to hold onto the bull with. He'd figured his best strategy to hang on was to rely on brute strength, rather than on the artful flopping backwards and forwards with one arm in the air like the other guys did. He thought that looked sissy. But his strategy had failed. The bull was the bigger brute.

What a surprise. I realized the futility of saying anything about his decision-making process or the obvious results.

Matthew winced and whistled air through his teeth as Daddy examined his arm, but then said proudly, "3.9 seconds, Doc! I rode him for 3.9 seconds!"

Daddy had Alma take a Polaroid of his arms, the most gorgeous biceps for miles, and put the photo on the bulletin board where we displayed the various sorts of gruesome warnings the government insisted we post. I looked at it every time I went up or down the hall.

But I really didn't need the picture as a reminder because the next day Matthew came in again, this time complaining that his ribs hurt. When he told me what was wrong, I shook my head. Alma x-rayed his ribs. We were all relieved to learn that nothing appeared broken. Daddy took pity on him though and strapped him into a corset-like rib brace that would reduce the range of movement in his chest so it would hurt less to breathe. Excessive manliness cured by wearing a corset. There was cosmic justice in that.

Matthew came in *again* the day after that, really embarrassed this time, and showed Daddy (but not Alma or me) an enormous bruise that covered the side of his lower body, centered on his hip and thigh. It obviously resulted from his impact with the ground after the bull sent him airborne.

As he was leaving, Alma asked Matthew if riding the bull had scared him. He admitted it had and said the really hard part had been climbing up the outside of the pen to get on the bull's back.

"It took everything I had to climb up there. I kept wonderin how I'd gotten myself into such foolishness. I prayed, 'Lord help me make it to the gate. And help me look like I know what I'm doin.' I'z standing across the top of the fence, supposed to get on the bull, but I had no idea how to do it. I asked the fellow that was holdin onto one of the ropes, 'What am I supposed to do?' He said, 'Just try to sit on the bull's back and you'll see.' Then another fellow said, 'You'll need to lean. He's a lurcher.' I was wonderin what that meant when they opened the gate. Then I found out."

A few days later I discovered that the miners who'd paid Matthew's entry fee had also made a videotape of his ride. I called the personnel office to ask if we could borrow it. Darla said, "Sure, but you gotta wait your turn. It's a real hot item around here."

I bet it was.

I thought about Matthew's mid-life crisis. He was facing the loss of physical strength and athletic ability, worrying about missed adventures. But he'd dealt with his worries bravely, head-on, and suffered the consequences as gracefully as he could. I guess that's the best any of us can ever do.

"My nurse told a female patient, 'Strip to the waist and put this over your head.' Then she handed the patient a folded paper gown.

"A few minutes later I came into the room and the lady was sitting on the examining table stripped to the waist, with the gown, still folded in a small square, laying on top of her head."

The Good, But Confused, Samaritans

A friend of mine who is a clinical psychologist said, "The thing that puzzles me the most about these stories you love is that nobody in them ever seems to have the brains or self-awareness to feel ashamed. They do something wacky, but then don't have the slightest hesitation in admitting it. The people in your community seem to utterly lack the capacity to feel humiliated."

That in a nutshell characterizes the people of the Southern Appalachian Highlands. We refuse to be embarrassed just because we made a mistake, even a really big mistake.

East Tennessee is an area where life has been so difficult for so long people have learned the value of an awkward situation. In a place where everyone is poor, human foibles are prized as an endless supply of free entertainment. Inhabitants of the Smokies love to tell silly stories on each other.

Ulysses, the courier from the local pathology lab, came by

Daddy's office to pick up whatever biological specimens we collected and take them to the hospital in town to be analyzed. He was an elegant Black gentleman with a wonderful sense of humor who'd been coming by nearly every day for years. He was like a member of the family.

One day he came in and plopped down on the stool in the lab area wearing a wrist brace. "What happened to you?" I asked.

"See that nice new van out there?" he said, pointing out the waiting room window.

I nodded.

"I totaled the other one yesterday."

"Oh goodness! How bad did you get hurt?"

"Not as bad as people thought I had," he said, laughing.

"What happened?"

"I was on my way to make a pick-up at Dr. Reynolds' office and a big dog ran out in front of me. I swerved to miss him and got a wheel off the edge of the pavement. I jerked the steering wheel to try to get back on the road, but that didn't work out. Anyway the van turned over. And over and over. I don't know how many times. A lot.

"I ended up laying on my left side against the driver's door. The van was on its side in somebody's flower bed. I had my seat belt on so I didn't get hurt, except for spraining my wrist," he said, as he brandished his brace.

"Wow," I said. "You were really lucky."

Ulysses nodded ruefully, then continued. "The wreck threw specimens everywhere. A lot of the containers broke and spilled out all over everything. I was covered with stuff I don't even want to think about. I started to climb out through the passenger door—which was straight up overhead—but then I remembered I'd laid my billfold on the seat when I got in the van that morning because it's got so much junk in it, it's uncomfortable to sit on. Well of course it had gone flying along with everything else. But I knew the police would wanna see my driver's license first thing, so I needed to find it.

"I was digging around in the mess when the fellow whose yard I'd ended up in came out to see what was going on. I saw him look at me through the windshield and then take off running. He went to get his neighbor I guess, because the next time I looked up there was two of them. They were both staring at me bug-eyed. One of them hollered, 'Hang on! We've called the rescue squad and an ambulance!'

"Well, hell, that was silly. I wasn't hurt very bad and I didn't think I'd need much help, if any, getting out. But I wasn't going anywhere 'til I found my billfold, so I kept rooting around looking for it. I saw the two fellows talking to each other and gesturing, but I didn't pay any attention. Next thing I know they've climbed onto the van and are opening the passenger door. They look down at me and all the mess, but I'm still not paying much attention to them because I hadn't found my billfold.

"By this time the whole neighborhood has showed up. Some of them were moaning and carrying on. I thought that was pretty strange, unless it was the lady whose flowers I'd just torn up, but then it dawned on me that they were seeing blood spilled everywhere and they thought it was mine! They thought I was bleeding and I guess they thought I'd peed all over everything too because the urine smell was really strong.

"And these two clowns on top of the van were really

determined. I looked up and told them, 'I'm okay. I just need to find something before I can get out of here.'

"They were staring at me in this really odd way. I was squatted down, partly covered in all the mess, rummaging around. What I didn't realize was that an amputated leg I'd picked up at the hospital in Morristown had been thrown against the dash and was laying there halfway out of its wrapping. Everybody could see it through the windshield. They thought it was mine! Never mind that it was a white man's leg!

"One of the men said, 'Don't worry, we're gonna get you out.'

"At the time I didn't know what this guy's problem was, but he must've thought I was in shock or something and was picking through the trash looking for my leg! He decided to pull me out by force. He leaned down through the passenger side and grabbed at my arms, but I wasn't ready to get out! I started hollering and wrestling with him. Then his buddy leaned in started pulling on me too.

"Between the two of them, they hauled me out of there, with me fighting them. When they got me out, they saw I had two good legs."

"That musta been a letdown for 'em," I asked.

"Oh no! Things got much worse when they realized the leg on the dash wasn't mine."

"Why?"

"They thought they'd caught a serial killer! A guy driving around with a van full of body parts! It was awful. Things got ugly."

I laughed until tears were streaming down my face.

"Thank goodness the police got there quick—and had a sense of humor. Cause there I was, a Black man covered in blood and stinking to high heaven of pee, driving around with a white man's leg on the dashboard." He sighed and shook his head.

"Oh well, you know what all this means, don't you?" he asked.

"What?" I said, still laughing.

"All that work you did yesterday, anything involving specimens, you're gonna have to round everybody up and ask them to come back in so you can do it again."

Daddy was amazed at how quickly a patient mastered the difficult process of learning to speak again after having his larynx removed in cancer surgery. It usually took months, but this fellow did it in a matter of weeks.

When Daddy asked him how he did it so fast, the man replied, "I got ten kids and I cain't write!"

Groundhog Day

I've never seen any merit in the supposedly deep philosophical quandary that asks, "If a tree falls in a forest and there's nobody around to hear it, does it make a sound?"

Of course it does. How self-centered can you get? What kind of people think nothing could possibly happen in a place unless a human happens to be there?

Whoever these "philosophers" are, they should move here and maybe they'd get some real insight. In the Smokies it rains a lot, which makes for profuse vegetation. And we have hundreds of square miles of trees growing on steep hillsides. When these trees get tall enough to put a strain on their roots and it rains some more and maybe the wind blows at sixty miles an hour as it often does, they fall. Whole sections of forest will topple and a tangled wall of full grown trees will go roaring downhill in a landslide.

I feel sure it makes a mighty racket every time, regardless of whether any philosophers are there to hear it or not. Anybody who's ever hiked in the mountains can ponder this issue when they're confronted by a twenty foot tall jumble of debris strewn across the trail they're trying to walk.

This constant downhill migration of water and dirt and trees and whatnot can make it hard to keep your yard looking nice. And sometimes the mess gets even closer to home than your yard as I learned from Dr. Evans in this uniquely comical worst case scenario.

"I spent my first years as a doctor in Harlan, Kentucky. It's hard to believe the things you used to see there, the way people used to live, especially in the coal mining areas.

"Once I was called out to attend to a woman who was having a baby. She lived in a one-room house with a dirt floor. Actually, it wasn't dirt, it was mud. It was spring and had been raining a lot and mud from outside had run in under the walls right into the living area.

"Can you imagine walking around in mud inside your own home? I was shocked. I hadn't known that people lived in conditions like that.

"I approached the bed where the woman was laying and I was confused by the way the linens looked. The bed sheet seemed to be made of leather. I touched it and realized it wasn't actually leather, it was cloth, but it was stiff with filth. I don't think it had ever been washed.

"The bed, an old coal stove, and a bag of beans were the only things in the house.

"I asked for some water and the woman's husband, a man with a beard and long, dirty hair, brought me some water in a pan that had gravels in the bottom of it. They simply didn't have any concept of sanitation.

"The woman made a moaning sound and I moved closer to

the bed to examine her but I was suddenly attacked by a pack of giant rats that came crawling out from under the bed.

"I kicked at 'em, but I couldn't fight 'em off, there were too many of 'em. They were biting me on the ankles and shins! It was disconcerting to say the least. Every time I tried to get close to the woman, I got attacked again.

"The creatures had fierce teeth, too. Their bites were drawing blood.

"I shouted at the husband to do something, to help me.

"He just stood there in the mud, smiling, and said in a slow drawl, 'They's nothin more triflin than a pet groundhog,' and never lifted a finger to keep them away from me.

"It was a great relief to learn that the beasts weren't rats, but groundhogs. And that they were the woman's pets.

"She had a family of pet groundhogs living in a dirt burrow underneath her bed. And they were attacking me because they were trying to protect her. Whenever they heard her cry out in childbirth and saw me come near, they tried to chase me away. They were far more concerned about her wellbeing than her husband was.

"I got attacked several more times during the delivery, but the ferocity of it tailed off significantly.

"Despite all the chaos and the primitive conditions, the delivery went fine. I've never been so happy to leave a house in my life as I was when that was all over.

"I've always remembered that man's remark and it makes me smile every time I think of it, even fifty years later: 'They's nothin more triflin than a pet groundhog.' Well, . . . nothin but that woman's husband."

"Well, he failed everything but his temperature!"

– said by Susie Harrell Shorbe, Daddy's nurse, as she came out of an examining room.

The Wood Butcher

The Great Smoky Mountains are the oldest mountains in the world. Geologists say the earth's growing pains have raised the Smokies up higher than the Himalayas more than once and the weather's worn them back down again to the deceptively soft looking blue and green corrugations we see today.

These rounded lumpy mountains are one of most biologically rich places on the planet. An extraordinary diversity of flora and fauna exists in these particular mountains because, unlike the Alps and Himalayas which run east to west, the Smokies run north to south. So when ice ages came and went, plants and animals were able to retreat and advance as necessary. There was no mass extinction of species from being trapped between a rock and a hard place or, to be precise, between a glacier and a mountain as happened in Europe and Asia.

It's a little known fact, but the woods in parts of the Smokies are high enough and wet enough to be classified as rainforests or even cloudforests. And what looks from a distance like a sleepy blue washboard, is actually a lethal environment of sheer rock cliffs and steep hillsides made impossibly slippery by deep carpets of fallen leaves. It's a place where watersheds are periodically ravaged by flash floods, denuded by avalanches of mud, or buried under walls of debris containing the tangled remains of fallen forests. And if these hazards aren't enough, the lush wilderness is interspersed with jungles of rhododendron and mountain laurel so impenetrable they're called *hells* by the locals.

This sort of terrain can make it tough on people trying to get to a doctor or vice versa.

A patient displayed his left palm and pointed out a scar across the base of the little, ring and middle fingers. "Doc sewed three of these back on more'n twenty years ago," he said, wiggling his fingers. "See, they all still work real good."

I smiled.

"They got cut off when Daddy and I were runnin our woodshop."

"I didn't know you used to be a wood butcher." He'd run a small restaurant as long as I could remember.

"Oh, it was a part-time thing. We were gonna make oak tables on the weekends and were settin up a shop in an old rundown place on the highway, down near the Saddle Rack."

The Saddle Rack was the local bar. A tiny dive that defiantly managed to eek out an existence in the dead center of a colony of hard core Baptists.

"I was movin some of my equipment around and had a router in my hand when Daddy saw a loose power cord and plugged it in! The damn thing came on and sawed off half my hand before I could let go."

I winced at the vivid image.

"Daddy tied his shirt around my hand to try to stop the bleedin, but it was still gushin. We ran outside and hopped in our truck, but the old thing wouldn't start! It was like that sometimes.

"So, then we run over to the Saddle Rack to see if we could find anybody there at nine in the mornin. They was still a few customers left over from the night before. Daddy hollered out that he needed somebody to run me to Doc's right quick. A friend of Daddy's was settin in the back and he said, 'I'll take ye!'

"We went outside with him but we couldn't find his car.

"Then he remembered he'd got a ride the night before and hadn't drove hisself. So we went back inside and asked again and a lady at the bar said she'd take us. She was drunk as a sailor, but we had to let her drive cause she said we was strangers and she wasn't lettin no stranger drive her new car."

"I prayed the whole way. Her drivin ride scared me worse than thinkin I might lose my fingers. But we made it! And Doc put 'em right back on!"

"They told me I had multiple cirrhosis."

Losing My Patience

Everyone loves the idea of belonging somewhere. Whether it's a quaint small town or a big happy family, the idea of being part of a loving community, or the idealized fantasy of it, is mighty attractive these days.

But the reality of living in community is that it takes at least two people who will put up with each other. It's a lot easier to think benevolent and charitable thoughts about humanity in the abstract without having to back it up with any face-to-face interaction. This is why the Lord had to spell it out for us by saying *love thy neighbor*. Anybody can love the poor people who live half way around the world, but it's a lot harder to be nice to the people you see everyday.

Hell is other people, as some French guy said. But so is heaven. Life is such a paradox.

Harley Hawkins was a good example of this predicament. He was a loveable guy with a noble, even heroic character. He worked one of the most terrifying jobs in the world.

He was a specialist at sealing leaks in mines. He went all over the world and fixed metal or gem mines where they'd accidentally drilled into a river and water was thundering in at a rate of a million gallons a day, or an hour.

Harley would descend a couple of miles underground and wade around 'til he got the leak fixed. I always thought of him as the Little Dutch Boy From Hell. Harley loved his job. Unfortunately there wasn't enough work to keep him busy seven days a week. And he wasn't the kind of fellow who dealt well with boredom, so if he had a lot of free time he drank.

Drinking transformed his naturally brave nature into reckless, accident prone lunacy. Harley almost never got injured on the job, but he got hurt so much when he was drinking that sewing him up became a life's work for Daddy. We made so many house calls to the Hawkins place, I learned to drive in their long dirt driveway.

One night Daddy took me with him when he went to Harley's in response to a desperate call from Avon. I waited in the kitchen with her while Daddy went back to the bedroom to assess the situation, but we could hear everything that was being said.

"Whad'ya get into this time?" Daddy asked.

"Doc," Harley said in a slurred voice. He was obviously bombed. "I been dry nearly a week. Then me and Avon went to the fair."

Oh Lord, I thought, Harley at the TVA & I Fair. The potential was mind-boggling.

"We seen the chickens and the rabbits and was restin before takin a look at the cattle. I'z eatin a cherry slushie when some guy splashed a drink on me." Harley let out a huge sigh. "It must've been the devil hisself that done it, because that liquor went all over me like fire. I could feel that drink run up my arms and then all the way down my legs. I couldn't hold myself back after that."

I crept down the hall and took a peek into the bedroom.

Harley was lying down and Daddy was sitting on the edge of the bed sewing up a gash on his forehead. He'd passed out and hit his head on something when he fell. In strong light Harley's forehead looked like Frankenstein, but Daddy always worked on him with the care and delicacy of a plastic surgeon.

Daddy waved me into the room and had me stand nearby so I could hand him supplies. When he finished sewing, Daddy said, "Now you stay here, Harley. I'm gonna go talk to Avon for a minute." Then he got up, and I followed him into the kitchen where he sat with Avon to commiserate and have a cup of coffee. We'd been at the kitchen table a couple of minutes when we heard a crash.

It was Harley, of course. He'd gotten out of bed and tried to eavesdrop on what was being said. He'd been holding himself upright by sliding along the wall. He'd made it most of the way down the hall, but then he'd come to the opening for the door into the bathroom. He'd fallen through it, hit his head on the tile floor, and torn open the cut on his forehead that Daddy'd just sutured.

That made Daddy mad. Really mad. He stood over Harley, hollering down at him as he bled onto the bathroom floor, "Good Lord, Harley, what'd I just tell you? I can't even get out of the house without you cutting yourself again! Well Mister, I'm gonna fix this problem right now."

He grabbed Harley by an ankle and dragged him back to the bedroom. Then he wrestled him back onto the bed. He called out, "Avon, have you got an old sheet?"

She brought him one and he ripped it into four strips. He tied Harley spread-eagled to the bed with the shredded sheet. Harley didn't resist. He just mumbled apologies to Daddy for making him mad.

As I looked down at Harley's tied wrists, the limits of medical intervention became clear—when a life-threatening addiction met a determined doctor, the best answer was forcible restraint. Tie 'em up.

Daddy sewed Harley's head up again and, as we left, he made Avon promise not to let him loose until he'd sobered up.

"When I woke up this mornin
I felt so good I thought I'd passed away!"

Happy Holidays

"When I was young I got stuck working at a drugstore in downtown Knoxville on Christmas Eve. Business was very slow. In the wee hours I heard someone come in the front door and looked up to see a naked lady, obviously mortified, and desperate for help.

"I had no idea how she'd gotten into the situation she was in, but, of course, I wanted to help her. We didn't sell any clothes or blankets or anything like that in the drug store, so all I could think to do was tear open a roll of Christmas paper and I wrapped it around her as quick as I could.

"She'd been crying, but we both started to laugh when we saw her wrapped up like a Christmas present.

"It turned out she was a prostitute who'd been picked up by a man near the University of Tennessee and then kicked out of a moving car without a stitch of clothes.

"Who would do a thing like that? And on Christmas Eve.

"I called a friend for her and they brought her some clothes and took her home."

"Every Christmas I think of that lady and hope she's alright.

"Holidays are just as awful in the Emergency Room.

"You see everything. It can be funny or terrifying, or sometimes it's funny *and* terrifying at the same time.

"I was working in the ER one night when a drunk fellow was brought in. As soon as I drew back the curtain on his little cubicle, before I could speak, he mumbled, 'Doc, I got an *awful* headache. You got anything for a headache?'

"On a hunch I asked him if he knew what might be causing his headache. He couldn't think of a single thing. He said he didn't get them often.

"The man had an ice pick driven into the top of his skull. Only the wooden handle was sticking out. When I mentioned it to him and asked him how that had happened, he was stumped. He had no recollection of being in either a fight or an accident.

"I was terrified to even touch the ice pick, so I called a neurosurgeon immediately and prayed he would be able to cure the fellow's headache without killing him."

"I've seen a switchblade embedded in a guy's head all the way to the hilt, too. That man was also walking around, talking. It made an unnerving sight, him standing there talking with that knife handle sticking out of the top of his head.

"And I've treated Sterno drinkers who'd poisoned themselves to such an extent that they no longer had even a blink reflex. They'd lay there on the gurney, eyes wide open, unconscious, and you could touch their eyeballs without provoking a blink. Then the next morning when I made my rounds they'd be sitting up in bed laughing and talking and eating the best meal they'd had in weeks!

"A normal person would *die* if they drank wood alcohol or got a piece of metal driven through their skull, but others barely notice a problem."

Doctors frequently get told things they don't believe. Dr. Kent told me he once examined a fellow in the Emergency Room who'd been shot nine times with a .22.

"None of the bullets were fatal, but he had holes all over him. He was talking and acting fine.

"I asked him, 'How did this happen?'

"He said, 'I was squirrel hunting and climbing over a fence when my gun went off by accident.'

"I said, 'You shot yourself nine times by accident?'

"He said he had.

"I later learned he'd been shot by a jealous husband while trying to escape from a house that wasn't his own."

Swept Away

I confessed to Dr. Samuels that Daddy had startled the occasional patient by operating on them with non-traditional surgical tools, like pliers, if he thought that would work better than bona fide medical instruments.

He agreed in principle with Daddy's approach and said he'd found that in emergencies, especially with certain types of patients, the low-tech solutions worked best. Here's the example he gave me.

"My second cousin was a drunk and a lawyer. And he was an idiot and a wildman. Everybody called him Tarzan.

"Once he had a terrible car wreck. He collided with another drunk, head on, and killed a man and woman.

"He was brought from the scene of the accident directly to my office, still out cold, which was lucky for him.

"It was obvious from looking at him that when the impact occurred, he'd been holding a bottle of liquor between his legs.

The bottle had shattered and cut him up something terrible. He also had pieces of broken windshield all over him.

"They say God looks out for children and drunks, and I guess he does because the liquor bottle shattering had the effect of immediately pouring alcohol over his wounds.

"He was bleeding quite a bit, but there was so much broken glass in his clothes and in the lacerations I had to get some of it off him before I could see to sew him up.

"I decided to use a broom.

"The only broom we had was the regular long handle broom we kept in the closet. I used it to sweep the glass fragments off him and into a dustpan. The rest I just brushed off into the floor.

"Then I was able to get the bleeding stopped and dress his wounds. He stayed unconscious the whole time I worked on him.

"He recovered beautifully, of course. It's amazing how tough some people are. Especially drunks.

"In fifty years, Cousin Tarzan's the only person I ever needed to use a broom on. I guess every family has one of these characters. One's about all you can stand."

"I spent 30,000 hours as an Emergency Room doctor here and elsewhere in addition to my regular practice," said Dr. McBride.

"One night they brought this character into the ER and he immediately grabbed one of the nurses and held her with a switchblade knife. He demanded narcotics.

"I said, 'Fine.'

"I pointed to a locked box nearby, held up a key, and said, 'I'll go to the narcotics box and unlock it with this key and get the narcotics for you.'

"It wasn't really the narcotics box. It was where they kept a pistol with a nine inch barrel.

"He let me go unlock the box and as soon as I got it open I jerked that huge pistol out and pointed it right between his eyes. I said, 'Put that knife down right now.'

"He put the switchblade down and said, 'Yes sir.'

"After that he was the sweetest thing you ever saw.

"He'd hurt his hand in a fight. I put the gun in my belt and x-rayed his hand.

"It was broken, so I fixed it.

"He behaved himself the rest of the night."

A friend complained that his brother-in-law had phoned and woken him up in the middle of the night.

The brother-in-law said, "I like to drink a few beers every night. Do you think I've got a problem?"

My friend said, "Well, I like to eat green beans every day, but I don't go callin people up at midnight to ask them if they think that means I've got a problem! So whadda you think?"

The Numbskull

Daddy knew all the people he treated. He knew several generations of their families and usually lots of their cousins, too. So he was never treating just a medical problem, he had to deal with the social and psychological setting the medical issue was embedded in. Sometimes that was a help, but sometimes it was just added frustration because he knew the best he could do was to patch 'em up and send 'em back out to get hurt again.

I remember the first time I ever saw a gunshot wound to the head. I was maybe ten, and went over to the office with Daddy in response to an emergency call one Sunday afternoon. On such a serious case Momma would normally have gone with him, but she was at the grocery store and this was long before the advent of cell phones.

I retain a perfectly clear image of Daddy standing bent over, silently scrutinizing the side of a man's head. His hands were partially visible through transparent gloves as they hovered in momentary hesitation, suspended in the brilliant light of the surgical lamp. He took a deep breath and let it out slowly as he selected another instrument from the array laid out on the stainless steel tray.

He'd been operating on Sterling Rader for most of the afternoon and I could tell he was tired. Sterling, a handsome dark-haired man in his early twenties, lay curled on his side on the operating table. His head and shoulders were covered with a light blue disposable sterile drape. Daddy had cut out a hole in the middle of the sheet so he could work through it and have a clean place to rest his hands.

Because of the drape I couldn't see how Sterling was holding up, but I could tell almost the exact moment that Shoun, his father, decided he was probably going to live, because he finally broke his long silence.

"Boy, you have done took the cake with this'n," he said.

Sterling's muffled retort came from under the sheet, "I didn't do nuthin."

"Well, I bet next time you'll think twice before ye light into your wife in her Daddy's front yard!"

Sterling lifted up a corner of the sheet with one bloody hand and peeped at his father in surprise. "Who told you that?"

"Her Daddy did when he hollered at me to come haul you outta his yard!"

"She's my wife!"

"She don't wanna be your wife no more. And you better not be goin over there again, or next time I'll shoot ye myself! I never seen any fools fight like y'all do. But I thought *even you* had more sense than to go to beatin her right where her Daddy could see ye."

It was a good thing that only I could see Daddy's face, because he was having a hard time keeping it straight during this exchange. I stood in the far corner of the room, chewing on my second Jumbo Tootsie Roll as I took everything in. From Shoun's remarks and what I'd seen earlier, I was now able to piece the story together.

Shoun had brought Sterling in with a t-shirt tied around his head. He looked like something out of a horror movie. His face and neck and chest were heavily streaked with wet and dry red rivulets. When Daddy untied the shirt to take a look, he asked, "Shotgun?"

"12-gauge," Shoun replied.

Daddy dropped the bloody shirt into the trashcan and reached up with his bare fingers to press on an artery near Sterling's temple that was spraying blood in time with the beat of his heart. Sterling was going to bleed to death if something wasn't done quickly.

Daddy pushed him down into a sitting position on the table and fumbled to open a sterile packet with one hand. He didn't take time to put on gloves or do anything else before he said, "Sterling, you're not gonna like this, but I've gotta put a stitch into you real quick without numbing you first. Okay? Hold real still."

Then he gritted his teeth and sewed a single deft stitch that pinched the artery closed. This done, he took a more considered look at the situation.

It was not good.

The whole side of Sterling's head was a dreadful mess. Daddy held a four-inch square gauze pad against the worst of it and turned to say over his shoulder, "Shoun, you've gotta take

Sterling to the hospital with this. He needs a surgeon."

"Can't Doc. He don't have no job nor no insurance. You just do the best you can and that'll be fine." He fished a plug of Beechnut tobacco out of the red and white striped pouch he carried in his overalls, put it in his mouth, and settled back to wait.

Daddy just grunted. A doctor practicing alone in a rural area came to expect this sort of thing occasionally. Especially considering East Tennessee's unparalleled passion for firearms and self help.

He laid Sterling over on his side and stepped on a floor pedal that automatically raised the table to a comfortable height while he worked his fingers into surgical gloves.

When most of the bleeding was stopped, he x-rayed Sterling's head to see how far the buckshot had penetrated. Luckily, Sterling had been moving when his father-in-law had fired at him and none of the shot had gotten any farther than his scalp. Not a single piece had penetrated his skull to reach his brain.

This being the case, there didn't seem to be anything left to do but to return to cleaning and sewing him up. Before he did that, though, Daddy had to empty several syringes of anesthetic into Sterling's scalp—making him quite literally a numbskull.

The heavy silence that had set in after Shoun's brief outburst was punctuated frequently by the ping of a piece of shot being removed from Sterling's scalp and dropped into a metal bowl.

When Daddy had patched things up as best he could, he wrapped a huge, white gauze bandage around Sterling's head, gave him some sample pain pills a drug company representative had left, and sent him out to wait in the car while Shoun settled up the account.

Shoun pulled his billfold out of the zippered pocket in the chest of his overalls and said with his mouth all lopsided from the wad of tobacco, "How much do I owe ye, Doc?"

I could see Daddy running up the tally in his head. Let's see, we had two cranial x-rays; facial and scalp surgery; tetanus, antibiotic, and anesthetic injections . . . .

Shoun wouldn't be able to afford even the cost of the supplies Daddy had used, much less anything for his labor. But Daddy had to be careful and not appear to be giving him charity. He needed to arrive at some figure that would seem exorbitant, but was within reach.

He gave Shoun a long, assessing look and said, "Fifty dollars."

Shoun winced and opened his billfold wide to show Daddy, "All I got is twenty-eight."

"That'll do it then."

And because he knew he'd have a tough time explaining these charges to Momma, he didn't record the transaction on the day sheet.

On the way out we couldn't help but notice Sterling, seated in his father's pick up, head bandaged like a Turk, locked in a passionate embrace kissing someone.

I blurted out, "Reckon that's his wife?"

Daddy nodded, held his hand over his heart, and said, "Sterling's brush with death must've brought them back together." Then he rolled his eyes. "Carolyn, some people never learn. We'll be seeing him again."

"I'd rather be old than be him."

"When I worked in Georgia, I made several house calls to a shotgun house that sat in the middle of a cotton field.

"The family never paid me a penny. I didn't really expect them to. But when they heard I was going to leave town, they called and asked me to come over.

"When I got out there they told me they wanted to pay me.

"I said, 'No that's not necessary.' But they insisted.

"Then, right in front of me, they opened up a large steamer trunk that was absolutely full of paper money. I was dumbfounded.

"They pulled out an assortment of bills of different sizes and denominations and paid me. It was Confederate money!

"They had an entire trunk full of banded, crisp new bills, but paid me, of course, with the most ragged bills they had.

"I framed the notes anyway and they still hang in my office."

The Amazing Coincidence

One of the most touching things about hanging around Daddy's office for forty years was to see his patients aging alongside him. During his internship and for a few years afterward the television show *Dr. Kildare* represented everything a doctor should be. In those days Daddy delivered babies at home and saw lots of children and young families. Patients had often teased him by calling him Dr. Kildare.

He was too old to be the doctor in the later television series, *Medical Center*, although he looked enough like Chad Everett to have played his elder brother. Then for awhile he got to be right in sync with *Marcus Welby*, except he had to see forty-five patients a day while Marcus seemed to have only one a week.

None of the modern doctor shows bore any resemblance to anything Daddy did—everything was too high tech and noisy and panicked. Honestly, I'd hate to be sick or hurt and have to go to any of the hospitals like the ones on television. It would be too stressful. I don't know how anybody could ever get well in places where everyone is shouting and screaming all the time.

In the later years of his practice, Daddy and a large proportion of his patients were old. Every few days someone would say, "Now Doc, you can't quit 'til after I die, okay? Promise me you won't retire 'til after I'm gone." He'd always try to comfort them by promising to stay in practice, but we all knew he didn't have much control over it.

The patients in their eighties and nineties had different sorts of medical problems from the younger ones. One day when I came back to the office from lunch I found Daddy standing at the Formica counter making notes in a chart. He had a gigantic purple plastic ballpoint pen in his hand that advertised the name of a drug company on the side. Pandora Shipe came in right behind me and said she'd just dropped by to tell him about an incident with her father, to see what he'd make of it. She was pretty upset.

Daddy treated the whole Shipe family: Shadrach, his brother Mose, and his daughter Pandora. Shadrach was about ninety. His wife, Vernie, had died ten years earlier and since that time he'd been living with Pandora.

The incident in question had occurred the previous Sunday when Pandora had asked Shad if he would like to go visit Vernie's grave. He said he would.

"I took him out to the cemetery and led him over to where Momma's buried. We stood there together and looked at her grave. Momma's got a double headstone with two hearts on it. One heart has her name and birthday and the date she passed away wrote on it. The other heart gives Daddy's name *Shadrach Shipe* and his birthday. Since he hadn't passed away, the date of his death's still blank.

"At dinner that night I asked him, 'Daddy, did you enjoy visitin Momma today?'

"He said, 'Uh huh.' Then he said, 'It really set me to thinkin, though.'

"So I said, 'What about?'

"He said, 'In my whole life I ain't never come across anybody else with the same name as me afore. Who would've ever thought that they was somebody else with my same name and, of all things, they'd end up buried right there next to my Vernie. Isn't that somethin?'"

I wanted to laugh, but I could tell Pandora didn't think it was funny. So, I sat stone-faced with the inside of my nose burning from the effort.

"Doc, why would he say somethin like that? What's wrong with him?"

Daddy looked at her kindly and said, "Pandora, he's *old*. We all get old. He's just gotten old."

"Is he getting that All Timers?" she asked.

Daddy nodded.

"Is there anything I can do?"

He shook his head.

When she was gone Daddy looked at me and said, "Carolyn, I don't ever want to get that old."

"What's your alternative?" I said. "It's not good."

"Well then, whenever I get that old, you be sure and tell me."

"I will," I said. "I'll shout it real loud so you can hear me."

"I appreciate that."

"But, you know, you probably won't be able to remember what I've told you anyway."

"Thank goodness," he said, as he shook his head, "Nobody wants to know they've gotten old."

"He didn't want anybody to know he was farmin the graveyard so he hid the tombstones and put some junk cars out there too."

Toilet Tongs

I was trying to find the Medicare code for sore toes, wondering if toes, like fingers, were designated as *index* and *ring*, when I heard Daddy groan, "Oh no." Then he pleaded in a soft voice, "Please don't stop in front of the office with that thing!"

I swiveled in my chair to see the Brush Grinder pulling up out front in his white Dodge pickup truck. There was a toilet sitting out in the open in the bed of the truck. It looked sort of redneck, but I wasn't sure why that would irritate Daddy. The Grinder was probably remodeling a bathroom and was just stopping by on his way home.

"Oh mercy, mercy," Daddy mumbled, hanging and shaking his head. He was actually blushing. This didn't make any sense.

I stared at him in confusion.

"It's his new *invention*. He wants to show it to me. He was talking about it at the last meeting of the Rabbit Hunters."

"He's invented a toilet you can mount in the back of a

pickup?"

"No," Daddy whispered, but further explanation was cut off because the Grinder was coming through the door.

The Grinder was a big man, well over six feet tall, broad shouldered and considerably overweight. He was witty, energetic, and always in a good mood. I looked forward to his visits.

"Hey Doc! It's your largest patient comin to call!" the Grinder boomed. "Still savin at least half yer patients I hope. Right now yer lookin sorta puny yerself. Aren't ye feelin good?"

"I'm okay," Daddy said cautiously.

"Well good! It looks like I picked a good time then. I was hopin to catch you when you weren't doin brain surgery so you could come out and take a look at my newest invention," he said. "I brung the demonstrator. Got her just out front."

"Yeah, I can see that you do," Daddy said.

"Well come on out and I'll fire her up for ye."

Daddy was red-faced with embarrassment, but the Grinder didn't seem to notice.

I went out front with them. The Grinder's truck had been modified since I last saw it. It now had a conventional white porcelain toilet mounted on a large metal box right behind the back window of the passenger compartment. The toilet was turned to face backwards, so anyone sitting on the seat would be looking toward the tailgate. And it rode tall. The toilet itself was in good shape, but up close I could tell that the seat had seen a lot of wear. It was discolored, flaking, and extremely unappealing.

The Grinder explained that the toilet was a full-size working mock-up. It had hoses running from the tank to a box underneath and he showed Daddy over and over how it would really flush. The noise of the repeated flushing attracted a crowd. That seemed to please the Grinder. It mortified Daddy.

With great ceremony the Grinder brandished a set of long curving metal pincers. "Toilet tongs!" he announced to his audience, as if that explained everything.

The crowd stood immobilized by uncertainty. I was relieved, though. The invention must be the weird looking tongs, not portable pickup truck toilets. But what were the tongs for? I didn't let myself speculate.

They were at least two-feet long, made of a silver-colored metal, and had handles like a gigantic pair of scissors. The blades were curved like two briar scythes laid side by side. They were wicked looking.

To Daddy's dismay, the Grinder proceeded to drop a toothbrush and a lady's costume jewelry ring into the toilet bowl. The crowd was pulled in for a closer look. Then he flourished the tongs and fished around for the ring and toothbrush, ultimately removing them both.

"Hey, Doc, iz that yer new outhouse?" a man called out from his car as he drove through the parking lot.

"Ha, ha, ha," Daddy strained the limits of his acting ability to appear amused. He stood attempting to admire the invention, discussing its merits and possible marketing strategies. I marveled at his patience and his poker face. But after about the tenth flush he'd had as much as he could stand and said he had to get back to work.

The Grinder was a smart man and endlessly optimistic, but I thought this particular idea might be a tough sell.

"Grinder," I said, "that's a serious tool. It takes up a lot of space. Where's the housewife supposed to keep it?"

"Carolyn, you've hit on one of the things I'm still workin on," he admitted. "Right now, I'm thinkin they'll have to stay in the garage when they're not in use."

"Planning an infomercial to sell em?" I asked.

"Yep," he said. "Just like Tony Robbins. And I'm tryin to git a meetin with Walmart. The way I figure it, my target customer is a Walmart shopper."

"I'd say you're right about that," I said.

Someone in the crowd asked him another question, and I used the distraction as cover to escape. As I went inside I heard another flush. Maybe I lacked entrepreneurial vision, but somehow I couldn't see Toilet Tongs doing the same kind of volume business as Thighmaster or George Foreman Grills. But I hoped for the Grinder's sake, I was wrong.

"A man was brought to my office by his wife. She told me he'd been struck by lightning and fallen off the roof of a two and a half story house.

"That's a heck of a fall, not to mention the lightning strike.

"I examined him and, except for a couple of small scratches, he seemed fine. So, I asked him to tell me what had happened."

"'I'z workin on the roof of my house,' he said, 'when a storm came along outta nowhere.'

"'Before I could get to the ladder, I'z struck by lightnin and went flyin. I got throwed onto some telephone lines and bounced on 'em like I'z on a trampoline, then got slingshotted over into the top of a big crepe myrtle. It wasn't strong enough to hold my weight, so I fell out of it onto a hedge and then rolled off into the yard.'

"'After all that I figured I'z dead, so I just laid there.'

"'A couple of hours later my wife come home and asked me why I'z layin in the yard. I told her I thought I might be dead. She said I didn't seem to be and helped me up. Then she brought me in here to get an official opinion.'"

Moonshine

"When I first moved to this area a fellow from a little place beyond Mountain City came in asking me if I'd be willing to come see his daughter at their home. The family lived more than thirty miles away. It was late and he couldn't give me directions for how to get there, so he said he'd come back and meet me at my office at 7:30 the next morning and take me there.

"We met up the next day and went on a tortuous journey. I could see why he couldn't give me directions. We had to go over both Holston and Iron Mountains.

"We got as close as we could get by road and then had to make the last part on foot. To get to his house, a little cabin, we had to walk across a huge field.

"When I examined the little girl I realized I couldn't do anything for her.

"I gave her a little something anyway, I don't remember what, because I had to do *something*.

"Then I came back to check on her two days later. That time I decided to try a little whiskey on her. I told her parents that I'd go to a liquor store and get something and come back, but they said I didn't need to, that they had some good moonshine.

"'Ours is better than that old stuff you buy in the stores,' they said. So they had me try a little bit of it myself and I had to agree.

"I couldn't think of anything else to give the girl. And she was too sick to try to get her to the hospital. It was an awful situation.

"She did alright, though. The little girl had to do most of it on her own, but she finally got well, with no help from me. She managed to recover with nothing but a little bit of high quality moonshine."

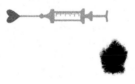

"I'm a hillbilly, but I ain't no redneck!"

– said by a woman whose husband embarrassed her by keeping goats.

Tough Choices

The Smokies are jam-packed with tree-sized evergreen shrubs of rhododendron and mountain laurel that turn the forests into a paradise of pink, white, and purple blossoms every spring. Aside from being the prettiest things in the mountains for a couple of weeks a year, they're a royal pain.

Rhododendron and mountain laurel roots and branches twist and interlace to form dense thickets covering many acres. These impenetrable tangles where neither man nor animal can pass are called *hells* by the locals.

If you don't understand what you're getting yourself into and suddenly discover you've wandered into one, it's hell to make your way out. You can't see or leap over them and you can't crawl under them. The best you can do it attempt to stay as high up in the tangle as possible by adopting a high-stepping gait or simply flinging yourself atop them in a something like a stage dive and crowd surfing at a rock concert. Here it's called rhodo surfing.

Even the best hiking guides will admit to having been caught in and tormented by them. We've all found ourselves in miserable situations where at some point we stop and wonder how we got into it. Doctors, too, sometimes find themselves in situations they didn't see coming

The responsibility carried by primary care doctors who work alone is immense. Life and death decisions are an all too common reality of their lives. And then they have to live the rest of their lives with the consequences of a decision made under stress and without much time to think. This is not an easy burden.

When I was about twelve, I heard Daddy come into the house in the middle of the night, and was surprised to hear him go into the kitchen instead of going to bed. That seemed strange. I got up to see what was going on and found him sitting at the kitchen table by himself. I figured this meant he was hungry so I decided to cook him the only thing I knew how to make, a sandwich from fried country ham. While I cooked it, I asked where he'd been.

I don't remember many of his exact words anymore, but his story burned a series of vivid images into my brain. He told me the safety director had called him to come over to the zinc mine to help recover a body. There'd been an accident. A twenty-three year old boy had taken a couple of steps backward into an area not illuminated by his helmet lamp and fallen off into a seventy-five foot deep mill hole that was used to dump mined rock down from one level in the mine to another so it could be taken to the mill to have the zinc extracted.

Statistics said a fall of forty feet was all it took to kill a man, so everybody knew the fellow was dead. Plus, the miners were such a close knit and intermarried community, the dead man was sure to have some family working on the same shift. Out of respect for them it was traditional to have a doctor come into the mine to recover the body.

It took Daddy about an hour to reach the site of the accident. He'd had to get dressed, drive five miles to the hoist, ride it straight down half a mile, and then make a long walk underground through the maze of shafts and be lowered on a rope until he reached the place where the boy had landed.

As Daddy neared the bottom of the hole, he began to hear a faint sound. By the time he reached the boy's side, he realized he was hearing the rattle of a man trying to breathe using lungs that were filling with fluid. It was a horrible wet sound and would only get more pronounced and erratic as the man drowned in his own blood.

The boy was still alive—at least for the moment.

Daddy swept the body with his helmet lamp. The injured fellow had landed like a rag doll across a pile of jagged rock. Daddy crouched over the inert, crumpled form. A quick examination revealed that the boy was unconscious and that the fall had surely broken both his feet, his ankles, legs, and his back and neck. If he lived, it would be as a quadriplegic at best. There was no way to know if his brain had been damaged as well.

Daddy knelt in the dark beside the gurgling unconscious form and tried to imagine the young man's future. He'd be confined to bed for the rest of his life. And he was only twenty-three years old.

Daddy hadn't bothered to bring his medical bag, since everyone assumed the miner was dead, so he had no stethoscope. He pressed his ear to the boy's chest and listened. His heart was strong. The left lung sounded almost clear, but the right one was filling with blood and burbling.

Daddy knew if he did nothing, in just a few minutes, the man would die. No one would ever know the difference.

He squatted, listening to the faint, erratic death rattles wondering what to do. If he didn't do anything, the boy would just slip away quietly, never knowing what had hit him. He wouldn't have to wake up with a live brain trapped in a dead body.

How could Daddy make a decision about something like this? How was he supposed to decide whose life was worth living and whose wasn't?

The Safety Director and several miners were walking through the long tunnel bringing a stretcher. Daddy could see the dancing lights from their helmets above him. One of them called out, "Doc? Did ye find him?"

Daddy was frozen with indecision. Should he try to save the boy? For what? What was the merciful thing to do? What was wise?

Then, without making a conscious decision, a lifetime of religious belief and medical training or maybe just pure instinct kicked in and he decided that such a choice was not his to make. That this choice belonged to God alone—so he rolled the boy onto his right side.

The gurgling slackened immediately. The blood was now running down into the damaged right lung, leaving the less damaged left side clear.

"Doc?"

Daddy sighed and stood up, letting his helmet light flash up toward the others like a beacon.

"He's alive!" he called out. "We're gonna need to be careful getting him out."

For nearly fifty years, Daddy's been tormented by that decision. The boy's young wife left him the day before he was sent home from the hospital, totally paralyzed. He spent the rest of his life, a couple of decades, confined to bed, first cared for by his parents and then by his sister.

I've often wondered what the right decision was. I still don't know the answer.

"I need a sip of Charlie Daniels."

Baptism & Resurrection

We've all seen that wives and mothers can be the most resourceful people on earth. They show us that even the most adverse circumstances can be faced and mastered with humble remedies.

This is especially true of rural doctors' wives. They get a lot of experience in emergency medicine and, in dire situations, might have to take matters into their own hands because the doctor is not around, or is unconscious, or maybe even dead.

The techniques employed by a desperate doctor's wife can be downright amazing.

After he retired, Dr. Williams and his wife Anne, who'd been a nurse, spent a great deal of time together at their home. He enjoyed working in the yard and she loved to read. One afternoon Anne realized she hadn't seen her husband in several hours. That was unusual. She went outside and called his name, but got no answer.

She walked through the yard calling his name until she heard a sound, but it was so soft she couldn't tell where it was coming from. She kept walking and called louder, "Where are you?"

Doctor Williams managed to mumble one last time, "Down here," then he fainted.

Anne found him lying in the driveway behind their split level house covered in blood. She didn't know what had happened to him, but he was still alive.

Anne was a small lady and her husband was too big for her to move. To triage him, she needed to find out where the blood was coming from. So she quickly got the garden hose from nearby and used it to rinse him off. When she got him hosed down, she could tell the blood was coming from his head.

She called 911 and in a few minutes could hear the ambulance coming, but then the sound of the siren faded and told her the driver was having trouble finding the right address. She heard him drive past the house at a distance a couple of times.

She continued to monitor the doctor's vital signs as they got weaker and weaker. Her husband's breathing and pulse faded to the point that Anne realized he was dying. But because she wasn't able to move him and wasn't sure exactly what the extent of his injuries was, there was nothing she could do. Then she lost his pulse altogether.

She had to do *something* immediately.

She did the only thing she could think of. She turned the water back on and hosed him off again, this time not gently with water that was warm from being in a hose that had lain in the sun all day, but with fresh, cold spring water.

Her strategy worked. The shock of being doused in cold water restarted his heart.

When the ambulance driver finally found the right house, the emergency technician was someone Dr. Williams had delivered, so he got especially attentive care.

It turned out he'd had a stroke and fallen off a five-foot retaining wall onto the concrete driveway below. He had to have thirty stitches to his head. And after he got out of the hospital, he had to use a walker for three years, but then he recovered enough that he didn't need it any more.

It seemed appropriate somehow that such a skilled doctor, a highly educated man with a long and downright heroic career, was saved in his own turn by a woman who was armed only with a garden hose.

"Tests on my eye showed everything's okay
except I can't see nothin."

The Premonition

On my way to see Dr. Taylor I got to see one of my favorite views in Tennessee. It's from the Interstate between Knoxville and Nashville, where I-40 runs along the side of a steep ridge and you can look down onto the city of Rockwood.

The town is in a four-mile wide strip between two sheer escarpments. The Sequatchie Valley runs in an almost perfectly straight line for 150 miles. It's a unique topographic feature in the world. The whole area gives off a strange and exhilarating vibe.

These sorts of landscapes mean there's often no other way to travel in the Smokies except by roads through dangerous areas like this. And country doctors have to drive them in the middle of the night, in all kinds of weather.

The lifestyle of a rural primary care doctor is so demanding, the entire family gets drafted to the extent they're willing and able to help. It's not unusual to hear about situations where a doctor's family rescued someone. Sometimes a whole community has to lend a hand. And sometimes it's the doctor who needs saving.

Dr. Taylor's wife told me about one of these situations.

"Once Sam went on a housecall way up in the mountains," she said. "I stayed at home with our children who were small at the time. I was painting the ceiling of the little house we lived in when all of a sudden I got the feeling he was in extreme danger.

"The feeling was overwhelming. I had two little children to take care of and he was out there somewhere in an old surplus World War II Jeep. I wasn't even sure where he'd gone. All I could do was pray.

"So, I got down off my ladder and prayed as hard as I could for a long time. I didn't stop until I felt he was going to be alright. But I never let on to the kids that I was worried.

"It was hours later when he got home. I told him about the premonition I'd had and told him that I'd prayed for him.

"He said he was looking for the house he'd been called to, driving the Jeep down a narrow road that ran along the edge of a cliff. He didn't realize it, but he'd made a wrong turn somewhere and had gotten on the wrong road. It was getting dark and suddenly the road he was on just dead-ended on the edge of a bluff.

"He started to back up, but the old Jeep didn't have back-up lights. He felt one wheel go off the dirt road, so he put on the brakes and carefully climbed out of the Jeep on the uphill side.

"He walked back down the mountain until he found some houses. Ten men brought ropes and went with him back to where he'd left the Jeep. They managed to get it hauled back onto the road and gave him directions to get where he was trying to go.

"And even though it was full dark by this time, he went ahead and made the housecall and was able to get back home safely.

"I thank God for those men who helped him," she said. "The Lord has protected us from the day we were married." She looked at her husband as she said this and they smiled at each other.

As I drove home, I mused about the times it was made clear to me, from the experiences of my own family and the many others I'd spoken to, that the arduous service performed by rural doctors would not be possible without the help of a strong relationship between husband and wife, and sometimes, as in this case, help from the community as well.

This, I think, is the most tragic loss brought on by the modern health care system. The loving interconnectedness of doctor, family, and community is being destroyed. These ties that bind us to each other are the bonds that define our humanity, and yet they are being systematically severed in the service of automated bookkeeping. The entire health care system is now being organized around machines instead of human beings. Not prioritized to reduce human suffering, but rather to optimize a computerized recordkeeping system. This is a tragedy.

"I felt so good when I got up this morning,
I almost got on the school bus!"

– said by an 80-year-old man.

The Shekinah

There's a miraculous cycle of light and life in the forest. As the seasons change, the same spot in the woods can undergo such drastic changes as to be unrecognizable from one week to the next.

When the foliage is at its most dense in summer, leaves block most of the light from the ground and obstruct the views. This can make the woods seem oppressive, even menacing. In fall when these same leaves give themselves over to a glorious display of color, the heart sings.

Then, in winter, when the leaves die and fall to the ground, breathtaking vistas are suddenly revealed that were never even suspected. And when spring comes, the sunlight shining onto the forest floor calls forth from the dull brown leaf litter a touching display of delicate wildflowers.

Eventually the leaves come out again to take their share of sunshine, gradually shutting out the light below and the cycle starts all over again.

Here's a story about a doctor in distress who appeals to a higher source for healing and experiences the miraculous power of light for himself.

Dr. Gregory was another of the rural physicians I spoke to who was trained as a specialist, but who chose to spend his life as a generalist instead. He conducted a busy office practice and established a small community hospital as well. When he fell victim to a debilitating medical problem that neither he nor any other doctor could cure, he was left with only one place to seek help.

"I had a *severe* neck pain fifteen years ago. I was wearing a neck brace and had to take strong pain medicine every three hours. It looked like it was a problem with a disc. I was in a terrible situation. I couldn't bear the pain, but was going to be a serious drug addict in short order if I had to keep taking medicine at the rate I needed it.

"I was going to have to quit practicing medicine. I didn't know what to do. I'd tried everything I could think of. I went to specialists, even the Mayo Clinic. I tried everything they recommended, but nothing was working. I was at the end of my wits.

"Finally my wife asked me to go and have the minister pray for me at the Methodist church. I wasn't a big church-goer, but I was utterly miserable and had tried everything else, so I went.

"I didn't have a lot of confidence in a Methodist healing service, so I didn't go up front at first. I sat on a pew in the back. Then the preacher started to pray and *immediately* I could feel the presence of the Holy Spirit. As he prayed, I couldn't help myself, I stood and walked up the aisle toward the front to where he was standing. As I walked I could see the preacher and I could see the people standing in the pews on both sides of me.

"Then the people faded out.

"I could see the minister and a laser-like light in a beam about a foot wide in front of me. The light was the brightest thing I've ever seen. It was as bright as a welding torch a foot wide and straight ahead of me. Then the preacher faded out and I fell in the floor.

"When I came to, I took my neck brace off and threw it in the floor and said, 'I don't give a damn what anybody thinks, I'm healed.' And I was.

"I've never had any trouble since."

Dr. Gregory fell silent, staring down at his hands, and his wife, who'd been standing behind him, leaning against the doorjamb between the living room and the kitchen said, "He was slain in the spirit and shown the Shekina light of God.

"I've known three people who've seen it," she said. "A little girl saw it when she was twelve years old and we were praying for her in the church. And when our own daughter was twelve, the minister saw it come down and cover her while she was praying in church."

Dr. Gregory nodded. "People can believe whatever they want to believe," he said, smiling, "but this is real. I know it's real."

"A doctor's reputation was very important in a rural community. They didn't trust outsiders *at all*.

"When I was first in practice, I wasn't doing very well until a family brought a man in who was passed out on moonshine. I waved some ammonia under his nose and revived him.

"The spectators were deeply impressed and told all their friends, so I got a reputation for raising people from their death bed. It wasn't true, but I was busy after that."

Dead Man Talking

Daddy got a call in the middle of the night about a patient of his who was on the way to the hospital in severe respiratory distress. It was a fellow he'd been taking care of for many years and this was the expected end of his chronic illness, but nevertheless, Daddy got dressed and drove to meet the man at the Emergency Room. When Daddy examined him, the man's lips were blue and he was having terrible trouble breathing.

He was so weak he couldn't move or speak. But he was conscious and his eyes were open, imploring.

Daddy said it was clear from looking at him that he was dying. He said he decided the best thing he could do for the man was "sit with him and hold his hand while he went to meet St. Peter."

While Daddy held his patient's hand a pulmonologist came by to see if he could help. The specialist tapped a line of pure medicinal cocaine onto the side of his left index finger and held it under the patient's nose. He told the sick man to try to breathe it in.

Cocaine was, and still is, an emergency astringent used to make it easier to get a breathing tube up a person's nose.

The sick man did the best he could and managed to snort a little of the cocaine into his system.

Then Daddy got to see a miracle. Even years later he still says he's never seen anything like it.

In a few seconds the man started smiling. Daddy said the fellow's lips were purple, but he let go of Daddy's hand, sat up on the gurney, and said in a strong, happy voice, "Doc, I think I'm gonna make it!"

It turned out he was wrong about that. He died a few minutes later with my father by his side, but he died without any further misery. Daddy said there was something terrifying about seeing a drug that powerful. A tiny amount of white powder was basically able to temporarily reanimate and utterly mislead a near corpse.

You can see why people would get addicted to it. Effective medicines can produce a wide variety of side effects, though. Some of them you never see coming.

When you're in the doctoring business a sad, but normal part of the day may include learning that someone you know has died. Sometimes this is expected, or at least not a big surprise, and sometimes it's a shock.

When Daddy told Momma that one of his patients in the hospital had died, she took the man's file out of the wall of active files, wrote *Deceased* across the name and at the top of the front page, and moved it to the far right lower corner of the files. It was our graveyard for files and it was a point of pride that the area was extremely small.

A few weeks after she'd marked a file this way she had her heart attack and I began to man the reception desk. On one of the rare occasions she had to be in the office to pick up medicine for herself she was standing behind my chair at the front desk when Jesse Johnson came up to register. I could hear her sharp intake of breath when he said his name.

Quickly she jumped back into the tiny alcove in the files where the man couldn't see her and she couldn't be seen by anyone but me. She looked panicked. I assumed this was just someone she didn't want to see, and began to look for his file. I couldn't find it. I asked him if he'd been here before and he said he had.

By this time Momma was hyperventilating in the alcove and it was clear something was very wrong. I asked her what was going on. She said, "He died! He died two months ago. What's he doing out there?"

I assumed this was another of the bizarre effects of all her post operative medicine and said, "Momma, it's okay. He's not dead. I just can't find his file."

"It's because it's in the *Deceased* section!" she said. "I'm telling you the man's dead. What should we do?"

I decided to humor her by looking in the *Deceased* files—and to my surprise, I found the man's file. When Momma saw this she dashed past me in a blur and ran to Daddy's private office in the back where he was dictating notes on the patient he had just seen.

"Paul, Paul, Jesse Johnson's out front!

"So."

"He's dead!"

"Oh goodness, what's happened?" Daddy said as he stood up.

"I don't know. What's he doing out there? How did he get out there?"

"How would I know? I've been back here." Daddy started walking toward the front.

"Don't go out there!"

Daddy looked at Momma and said, "What're you talking about?"

She repeated that Jesse Johnson was out front waiting to see the doctor, but that she knew for a fact he died and her paperwork confirmed it.

"What are you saying? That a dead man is trying to register?"

"I … I think so."

"Woman, if he's out front, and talking, he can't be dead!"

"But he was in the *Deceased* files! You told me he died and I marked him *Deceased*!"

"Then one of us must have made a mistake. Just because I said it or you wrote it down doesn't mean it happened. Only God can do that. I think you need to go back home and lay down. Now."

She withered visibly and seemed to realize that the she might've been wrong about a corpse trying to see the doctor this morning. None of us had ever seen Momma this way before.

This was Momma, the last bastion of no-nonsense rationality. The woman who had disarmed a patient who was waving a loaded gun. Daddy and I both stood with our mouths agape.

When she'd gone, I told Daddy, "Boy, that heart medicine

Momma's takin is so strong, I think it might be spreadin, and workin on somethin that's none of its business."

"My first year in practice I delivered twenty babies. I was paid for four.

"Then thirty-five years later a fellow came in and paid for his own delivery and for all his brothers and sisters. He'd gotten a good job up north and come back home to settle up his family's debts. He tried to pay me interest, too, but I wouldn't let him."

The Black and White Dog

The most unusual botanical features of the Smokies are called *balds*. These strange patches of high ground which are bare of trees are famous for their beauty in the spring when the wild azaleas are abloom. The balds are afire with an astonishing array of flowers in reds, oranges, yellows, pinks, and whites.

Scientists disagree about why the flora of the balds is so utterly different from that of the rest of the mountains. The locals believe they know why. They call the areas *Devil's footprints*.

A lot of places in the Smokies are named for the devil: Devil's Courthouse, Devil's Den, Devil's Chute, Devil's Creek, Devil's Branch, Devil's Bedchamber, Devil's Tater Patch, Hell's Half Acre Ridge, and a waterway named Styx.

The locals are known for their fanciful, mystical thinking. Doctors, on the other hand, are trained to be scientific, even when they're around people who are *in extremis* where you can see plenty of strange things. On rare occasions doctors witness a miracle, but more often they see things they simply don't have any explanation for. This is a story about one of those times.

Dr. Andrews was raised in one of the most sparsely inhabited, inaccessible areas of the Smokies. An area so remote, the doctor couldn't get to some of his patients even with a Jeep, but had to travel on horseback or foot.

He went away for college, medical school, and an internship. But then, as soon as he could, he came back home to the mountains to practice.

He was a tall, muscular man with a ready smile and kind eyes. He told me wonderful stories about the years he spent working alone. But then gradually the area grew in popularity as a vacation spot and other doctors moved into the community, and then together they managed to get a small hospital built.

"There weren't many Black people living in the Smokies back in the '60's, but there was one gentleman, Mr. Jeffers, who lived on a small farm across the street from the hospital. I don't know how he came to be in the area, because as far as I know he had no wife or family anywhere near here.

"He was a tall, friendly, handsome man who had beautiful manners, but he kept pretty much to himself, working and living totally alone. Then, when he was in his 80's he suddenly acquired a mixed-breed black and white dog.

"He loved to tell people how Dan just showed up on his porch one day, well fed, bright-eyed, his fur shining. After that, they were inseparable. Anywhere you saw old Mr. Jeffers, you saw Dan.

"Mr. Jeffers had bad heart disease. As he neared his ninetieth birthday, he was in and out of the hospital many times. The rooms in the heart ward were two stories off the ground, but every time he was admitted to the hospital, his dog Dan somehow figured out what room he was in and came across the street and sat outside the correct hospital window.

"For however many days Mr. Jeffers was in the hospital, his dog would wait faithfully for him as close as he could get, looking up toward the window of his room.

"Nobody could understand how the dog did it. He wasn't able to see Mr. Jeffers through the window, because the man was strictly confined to bed, but somehow that dog knew right where his owner was.

"Everybody noticed him. You couldn't help but be touched by the total devotion of the little creature. When Mr. Jeffers died, the dog was sitting right below the window of his room, patiently waiting.

"I don't know what happened to Dan after his owner passed away, but for years and years afterwards, whenever someone was getting ready to die in that hospital, they'd report seeing a black and white dog in their room. It didn't take long for me to realize that any time a patient said they'd seen the dog, they were going die the next day.

"This happened over and over—twenty to thirty times that I know of. It happened to people who'd never heard the story about Mr. Jeffers or Dan! Very sick people who hardly knew what world they were in would see the black and white dog and talk about it.

"At first it happened only in the hospital and then it began to happen in the nearby nursing home. After a few years, it was mostly happening in the nursing home. Mr. Jeffers had never spent a day in the nursing home.

"I'm not a superstitious person. I don't even believe in things like that, and yet I know from first-hand experience that it happened many, many times."

Doctor Andrews stopped speaking, but he looked at me with a question in his kind eyes. I knew we both wondered what sort of creature it was that was able to help so many people across the border from life into death.

"How are we ever gonna find another doctor that don't wanna make no money?"

– asked by a woman whose large family hardly ever paid for any of their many visits to Daddy's office, when I told her Daddy was going to retire.

This book is dedicated to real life heroes

Dr. Donald H. Bradley

Dr. Larry Dorsey

Dr. Waverly Green

Dr. James W. Hedden

Steve Leeds for Dr. Horace M. Leeds

Dr. Robert W. Morris

Dr. E. P. Muncy and wife Jean

Dr. Billy Sams

Dr. Walter C. Shea

Dr. William N. Smith

Dr. John L. Sonner

Dr. Kenneth C. Susong

And

Dr. Paul L. Jourdan

Elise G. Jourdan, Pharm.D.

David C. Jourdan

About the Author

A former U.S. Senate Counsel to the Committee on Environment and Public Works and the Committee on Governmental Affairs, Carolyn Jourdan has degrees from the University of Tennessee in Biomedical Engineering and Law.

Carolyn lives on the family farm in Strawberry Plains, Tennessee, with many stray animals.

Her first book, *Heart in the Right Place*, is a *Wall Street Journal* bestselling comical memoir. It's a true story about a spoiled, high-powered Senate lawyer (Carolyn) who gives up a glamorous life in Washington and comes back home to the Smoky Mountains to work as an inept receptionist in her father's rural medical office.

It was voted the #1 Nonfiction Pick in the Nation, a Best Book of the Year, a Best Book Club Book of the Year, and a Most Fun Book Ever. It was also selected as *Family Circle* magazine's first ever Book of the Month and awarded the *Elle* magazine Readers Prize.

She is also the co-author of the *Bear in the Back Seat: Adventures of a Wildlife Ranger in the Great Smoky Mountains National Park* series and author of *Out on a Limb*, a brainy Appalachian medical mystery.

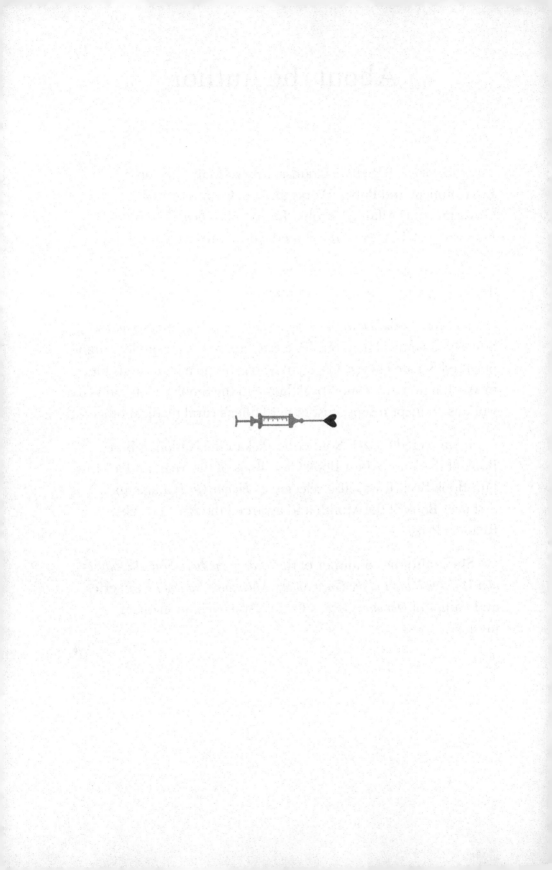

CPSIA information can be obtained
at www.ICGtesting.com
Printed in the USA
BVOW06s2103241117
501114BV00007B/11/P